NATURE'S SYMPHONY

LESSONS IN NUMBER VIBRATION

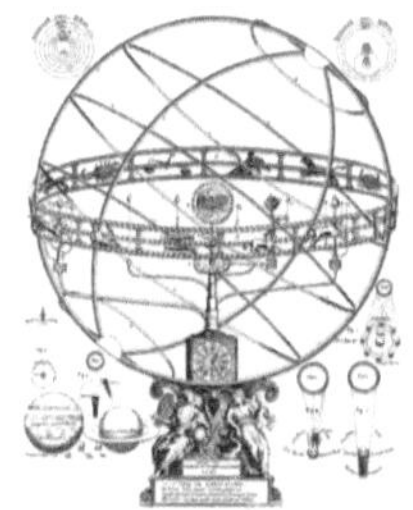

Some Other Titles From New Falcon Publications

Aha! The Sevenfold Mystery of the Ineffable Love **–Aleister Crowley**
Aleister Crowley and the Treasure House of Images
–J.F.C. Fuller, Aleister Crowley, Lon Milo DuQuette and Nancy Wasserman
Aleister Crowley's Illustrated Goetia, Sex Magic, Tantra & Tarot:
An Insider's Guide to Robert Anton Wilson **–Eric Wagner**
Ask Baba Lon **–Lon Milo DuQuette**
Bio-Etheric Healing **–Trudy Lanitis**
Diary of the Antichrist **–David Cheribum**
Enochian Sex Magic and How To Workbook
–Aleister Crowley, Lon Milo DuQuette and Christopher S. Hyatt, Ph.D.
Enochian World of Aleister Crowley **–DuQuette and Aleister Crowley**
Info-Psychology, Neuropolitique, The Game of Life, What Does WoMan Want?
–Timothy Leary, Ph.D.
Nonlocal Nature: The Eight Circuits of Consciousness **–James A. Heffernan**
Numbers Their Meaning and Magic Vol. I & II, Zodiacal Symbology Book I & 2
–Isidore Kozminsky
on What is **–Ja Wallin**
Rebellion, Revolution and Religiousness **–Osho**
Rebels & Devils; The Psychology of Liberation–**Edited by Christopher S. Hyatt, Ph.D.**
Reichian Therapy: A Practical Guide for Home Use **–Dr. Jack Willis**
Shaping Formless Fire, Seizing Power, Taking Power
Secrets of Western Tantra: The Sexuality of the Middle Path
Dogma Daze **–Christopher S. Hyatt, Ph.D.**
Steamo Goes to Havana, The Social Epidemic of Child Abuse
–Michael Miller, M.Ed., M.S., Ph.D.
The Illuminati Conspiracy: The Sapiens System **–Donald Holmes, M.D.**
The Magick In The Music and Other Essays **–Stephen Mace**
The Philosophy of Numbers, Vol. I & II, Nature's Symphony **Mrs. L. Dow Balliett**
The Psychopath's Bible **–Christopher S. Hyatt, Ph.D., and Jack Willis**
The Secret Inner Order Rituals of the Golden Dawn **–Pat Zalewski**
The Way of the Secret Lover Taboo: Sex, Religion & Magick
–C. Hyatt, Ph.D., and Lon DuQuette
The Why, Who, and What of Existence **–Vlad Korbel**
Undoing Yourself With Energized Meditation and Other Devices
Woman's Orgasm: A Guide to Sexual Satisfaction
–Benjamin Graber M.D., and Georgia Kline-Graber, R.N.

Other Titles by J. Marvin Spiegelman, Ph.D.

A Modern Jew in Search of Soul
Buddhism and Jungian Psychology
Catholicism and Jungian Psychology
Hinduism and Jungian Psychology
Mysticism, Psychology and Oedipus - A Small Gem
Protestanism and Jungian Psychology
Psychotherapy and Religion at the Millennium and Beyond
Psychotherapy as a Mutual Process
Reich, Jung, Regardie & Me - The Unhealed Healer
Rider, Haggard, Henry Miller & I - The Unpublished Writer
Sufism, Islam and Jungian Psychology
The Knight - A Small Gem
The Nymphomaniac
The Quest - Further Adventures in the Unconscious
The Tree of Life - Paths in Jungian Individuation
The Wisdom of J. Marvin Speigelman Vol. I - Selected Writings
The Wisdom of J. Marvin Speigelman Vol. II - Psychology and Religion

Other Titles by Dr. Israel Regardie

A Garden of Pomegranates
A Practical Guide to Geomantic Divination - A Small Gem
Attract and Use Healing Energy - A Small Gem
Be Yourself - A Guide to Relaxation and Health
Ceremonial Magic
Dr. Israel Regardie's Definitive Work on Aleister Crowley,
  The Eye In The Triangle
Healing Energy, Prayer and Relaxation
How To Make and Use Talismans - A Small Gem
Israel Regardie's The Foundations of Practical Magick
My Rosicrucian Adventure
Mysticism, Psychology and Oedipus - A Small Gem
Practical Magick - A Small Gem
Teachers of Fulfillment
The Art and Meaning of Magic - A Small Gem
The Body-Mind Connection, A Path to Well-Being - A Small Gem
The Complete Golden Dawn System of Magic
The Complete Golden Dawn System of Magic Book 1 - Ltd. Edition
The Complete Golden Dawn System of Magic Book 2 - Ltd. Edition
The Complete Golden Dawn System of Magic - The Black Edition
The Eye in the Triangle: An Interpretation of Aleister Crowley
The Golden Dawn Audio CDs, Vol. 1, Vol. 2, and Vol. 3
The Legend of Aleister Crowley
The Magic of Israel Regardie
The Middle Pillar
The Philosopher's Stone
The Portable Complete Golden Dawn System of Magic
The Tree of Life
The Wisdom of Israel Regardie - Vol. I
  Selected Introductions, Prefaces and Forewords
The Wisdom of Israel Regardie - Vol. II
  Selected Essays and Commentaries
The Wisdom of Israel Regardie - Vol. III
  Selected Articles, Introductions, Prefaces and Forewords
What You Should Know About the Golden Dawn
Wilhelm Reich, His Theory And Techniques
Aha! (Dr. Israel Regardie and Aleister Crowley)
Roll Away The Stone/The Herb Dangerous
  (Dr. Israel Regardie and Aleister Crowley)

ISBN 13: 978-156184-524-8

ISBN 10: 1-56184-524-8

New Falcon Publications First Edition 2023

The paper used in this publication meets the minimum requirements
of the American National Standard for Permanence of
Paper for Printed Library Materials Z39.48-1984

Printed in USA

NEW FALCON PUBLICATIONS
2046 Hillhurst Avenue
Los Angeles, California 90027
www.newfalcon.com
email: info@newfalcon.com

NATURE'S SYMPHONY

LESSONS IN NUMBER VIBRATION

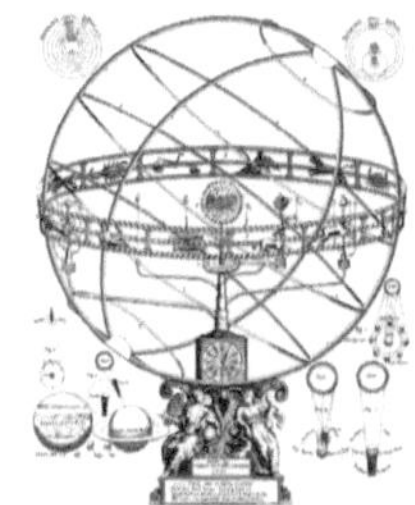

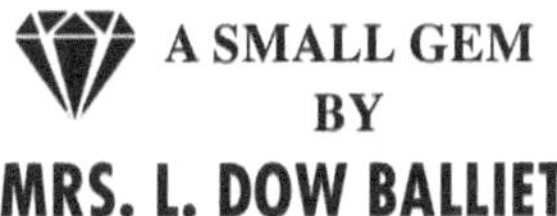

A SMALL GEM

BY

MRS. L. DOW BALLIET

NEW FALCON PUBLICATIONS
Los Angeles, California U.S.A.

Contents

MRS. L. DOW BALLIETT

A MASTER OF VIBRATIONS AND NUMEROLOGY, FOUNDER OF THE MASTER NUMBER SYSTEM, WHEREBY THE NUMBERS 11 AND 22 ARE NOT REDUCED. MRS. BALLIETT COMBINED PYTHAGORAS' WORK WITH BIBLICAL REFERENCE.

HER STUDENT, JUNO JORDAN, HELPED NUMEROLOGY BECOME THE SYSTEM KNOWN TODAY AS PYTHAGOREAN. MANY NUMEROLOGISTS TODAY STILL BASE THEIR WORK IN REFERENCE TO THESE WOMEN OF THE CALIFORNIA INSTITUTE OF NUMERICAL RESEARCH.

This book is lovingly dedicated

to

L. DOW BALLIETT, M.D.

Comrade–Lover–Husband

–The Author

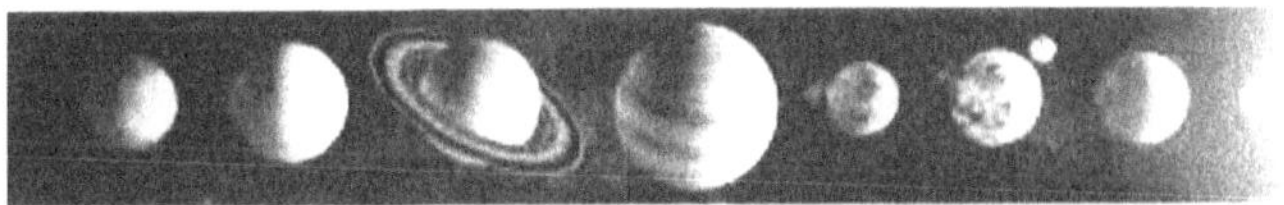

Preface

To comprehend these lessons scientifically the author would advise the student to first study the principles of Number Vibration found in the book *"Success Through Strength of Vibration: A System of Numbers as Taught by Pythagoras"* also "*Philosophy of Numbers; Their Tone and Color*," now available from New Falcon Publications.

Many systems of numbers have been developed from different sources, the Kabbalah usually being the basis. But every system is different from every other system. This, as you may know, has caused confusion and unbelief in the Science of Number Vibration. These lessons bring you a system of musical harmony in use today. It is founded, as all other systems are, upon the digit of numbers from 1 to 9. This is the correct teaching of Pythagoras, but from this point and finding the name and birth digit this system diverges from all others. If music has a scientific basis, then so has this system of Number Vibration, as it is built upon exactly the same foundation. Pythagoras, in the VI century before Christ, gave to the world his theory of the "Music of the Spheres" when he gave to the Greeks the fundamental principles of music now in use. If one part is true, this is true. You can prove to your satisfaction the basic principle of the One Source of all colors, sounds, and all things the eye sees, the ears hears, and the desire the heart longs for by the analysis of its mental structure. Each separate thing will speak up to you and tell you it's message if you will learn its universal language.

Mrs. L. Dow Balliett.

Atlantic City, New Jersey, U.S.A.

January 1, 1912

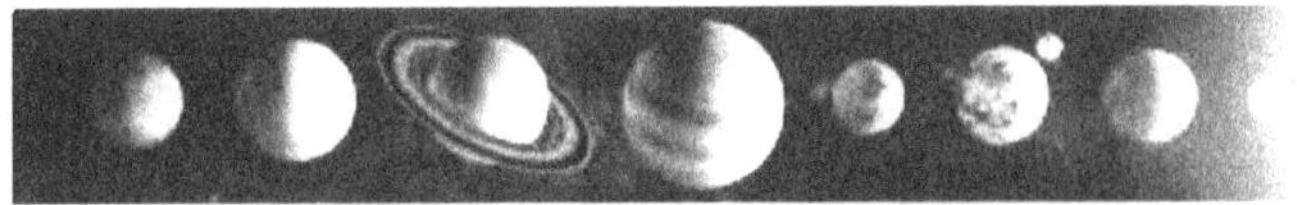

CHAPTER 1

The Name Or The Level of Consciousness

In all the Universe there is nothing at rest. Everything is in motion; all things from man to a grain of sand being in a constant state of vibration. But although everything is in motion, everything is not moving at the same rate.

The rate of vibration shows the quality of force that thing is using. The higher the rate of vibration, the greater the degree of spiritual force expressed.

The rate of consciousness the person or thing is expressing can always be told by the name the person or thing is using. Each letter of the alphabet has a certain value and these numbers added and the digit taken will tell the quality of force the thing is expressing.

Pythagoras used 9 rates of force, the digits from 1 to 9 expressing the different degrees of vibration. But in this century, because man has made some advance in spiritual knowledge, we add 11 and 22 to express the highest spiritual vibrations.

Pythagoras says every letter of the alphabet has its own rate of vibration and color. He divided numbers in this way:

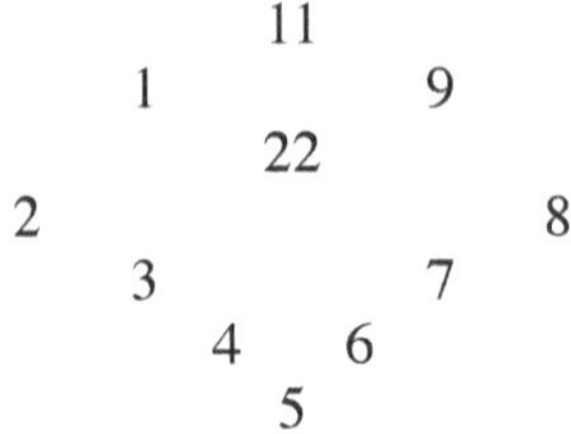

Into odd and even; into limited, and gave the preference to odd numbers. But we consider all of the necessary.

The system of numbers is founded upon Pythagoras' Ten Fundamental Laws of Opposites, which should be carefully studied, as they are the key. There are as many periods in one's life as there are parts in the baptismal name.

Read each part of the name separately; find its value according to the letters in the name. Then find the sum of the figures comprising each name and the digit. Read each period in regular order, according to the vibrations in each name. The digit of the whole name is the most important; as it shows the quality of vibration the person was born with, the now used, as how the world regards him at the present time.

To do this, find your birth vibration. This will show the part your higher nature wants developed.

To find your own numbers divide the alphabet into nine parts, thus:

1	2	3	4	5	6	7	8	9
a	b	c	d	e	f	g	h	i
j	k	l	m	n	o	p	q	r
s	t	u	v	w	x	y	z	

Now, although 11 and 22 express the highest rates, it is not true that 1 expresses the least spiritual force and the other numbers increase in spirituality in a regularly ascending scale. Quite the contrary is true. Each number expresses a certain kind of degree of force, and for man to be perfectly balanced it is necessary that he should work through all the numbers.

Some numbers hold their spiritual quality latent and outwardly express only material quality. But for man to be a perfectly developed, well-rounded individual, he must understand all the worldly truths expressed by the most material of the numbers.

We find in each vibration the minerals vibrating upon their own plane of consciousness as well as vegetables, animals and men. All vibrate in their conscious mental activity upon the plane to which they are related. Upon all planes there are different degrees manifested, which are expressed in the digits 1, 2, 3, 4, 5, 6, 7, 8, 9.

If we have vibration we must have sound, and if sound, also color.

Nature always acts through the Trinity of Substance, Force and Consciousness. The action of Substance and Force create the third motion, called Consciousness.

The force of liberated thought acts upon the children of men in a positive or negative manner according as they are attuned to the color and sound of the vibration.

The Cosmic Law speaks and acts through different expressions of the one Force according to the strength of its vibration, moving at its appropriate rate of speed. Moving at a certain rate, it has sound; at another rate, color.

Nature always acts through substance, force and consciousness.

We all know what is meant by substance; it includes everything that can be seen. We see only substance or so-called matter and may think of earthly substance as a spiritual thing vibrating at a very low rate of speed and far removed from its Divine Source.

Force we may define as the active foundation.

Consciousness shows what we can understand; it shows to what we are related.

Your name tells what you are, what rate of consciousness you have reached.

Notice the quality of consciousness expressed by each of your names and the rate of force expressed by the digit of the whole to know what power you have attained.

When an octave is struck a musician hears the intermediate notes forming the gamut of sound, while the untrained man hears only the high and the low notes. This difference shows their respective consciousness of sound.

One man sees a blue sky. It is blue and white to him; but another, whose color sense has been developed, sees red, yellow, blue, white and many shades blended into a harmonious whole. His consciousness of colors being greater, he is related to more colors.

One man sees the children of men as brothers, looking upon them as different expressions of the One Life, showing him to be in conscious relation with the Universal.

Another is consciously related only to those of his own blood, his consciousness of the Unity of all things being limited. It may be this last man is simply waiting for the door of higher consciousness to open; in which case some event will occur in his life which will force the truth to his notice. After he has reached the higher grade of consciousness he will make some change in the manner of his writing his name, which will show the advance he has made and lead to new environment.

In order to advance, to grow, one must work in the force and with the substances shown by the digit of the day, month and year of birth. This path contains the many experiences necessary to strengthen weak points and advance the growth of the soul in order to make what is called character.

Through this work we grow into higher relation of consciousness.

When a growth is actually made it will show in a change

in our name number, which will take a higher vibration or become more harmonious.

The digit of the name we use shows what we are at the time we use the name.

A person at one time in life will use certain initials and at another time another initial, or is known by another part of his name. This is not accidental. It shows the man as he is at the time he uses the name. His name expresses the rate of consciousness he is using at that time. He is vibrating to that especial chord.

There are as many periods in one's life as there are parts in the baptismal name, including the mother's surname before marriage.

The smaller sweeps of the pendulum are less notices, yet they may be making strong vibrations which will be expressed by different rates and numbers.

The name tells the wisdom you have already gained and which is now stored in your soul.

The name shows where the soul has arrived.

Men call this growth character.

The name records this growth of the soul.

The soul is a spiritual activity and it reaches out to its own intellect as master and compels the intellect to use a name representing its true self.

The intellect may deceive the soul never.

It is true many names bear the same vibration, as William and Elizabeth, which each vibrate 7. Yet the vowels differ, showing the spiritual desires of the possessors of the names are different.

The name is a true index of character, as the world will not recognize nor use a name which does not truly represent the person.

When soul and spirit act in unison the victories are recorded in the eternities, the Akashic Records–God's Book of Remembrance–keeping the permanent impression.

It is seldom a person is willing to change his name unless he has earned a higher vibration.

The vowels of a name show its spiritual structure–the desire of the soul reaches out in this way–and its leadings are generally embodied in the birth path, which shows the part of your system of body, soul and spirit which your higher-self desires to bring into expression.

The vowels in a name show the hidden desires which wish for expression.

The first vowel in a name is of principal importance, the others having a minor effect.

"A" stands for boldness of action and independent, fearless expression of what appears to be truth.

The action of this vowel, as of all the rest, is governed by the development of the person bearing it.

When two vowels are manifested in the same name, another channel of vibration opens.

The possessor of such a name will at one period of life vibrate to one vowel, while the other is held in abeyance and at another period to the other.

"E" is interested in everything in Heaven and Earth, from Black Magic to the investigation of the Creative Force.

"E" finds joy and truth through research.

"I" stands for the "I am" principle. It is the manifestation of spirit.

A person with this as his chief vowel is likely to seek advice from others, but after reasoning and thinking he is invariably controlled by the light coming from his own inner consciousness. Intellect and best judgment or it may be strong and evil as if emanating from Black Magic. It behooves any one with this vowel prominent in his name to realize that his body is the temple of the Holy Spirit and must be kept clean for his own soul's use, allowing no other spirit or force to enter.

The letter "O" is often found in the individual who appears to bear a contradictory nature; modest, but independent' strong, but appearing helpless. When a decision must be made it is made with judgment and reason. It is masculine in action and those bearing it will usually be governed by the father's bent of mind. "O" is slow in coming to conclusions when compared with the "I" people, who always know at once what they want and reason about it after deciding. But "O" cannot be moved after having made up its mind.

"O is always a money maker.

The last vowel, "U," represents the individual who in a sense stands alone.

He may mingle in the world, yet is never lost in the multitude.

He receives many gifts and favors, but holds them loosely. If he lives upon the highest plane of which he is conscious, others will come to remain.

Each of the numbers has a separate, distinct meaning.

No. 1

No. 1 is the binding chain, the Creator, the expression of Unity. All numbers possess this mystic vibration in latency. It is a chain of flame[1]–

6	3	1	4	5	= 19 = 1
f	l	a	m	e	

When you ask for light upon any subject, you call upon this creative principle, the 1.

When you call, the Divine within hears the call, no matter the force your birth digit shows you are using. The spirit of the 1 comes to your aid, kindles your light and with its flame changes a slower vibration into the one which holds the desire which has caused the cry.

Men call the 1 vibration crucifixion; but when it has triumphed 1 is not crucifixion, but triumph.

To conquer 1 must go when called upon any plane. To disregard the call means disaster to the individual's system of life.

To break engagements or to speak or act falsely means to break the unity of the whole.

---

[1] 6 + 3 + 1 + 4 + 6 = 19: 1 + 9 = 10; 1 + 0 = 1

When No. 1 understands that the law of life is Unity and starts from this point of contact, wealth and worldly success come to him.

A 1 person is apt to relate himself to the value of the vowels found in his name, as they show the hidden aspirations of the soul.

No. 2

No. 2 is the pivot upon which the first trinity of mind, 1, 2, 3, hinges.

This is the working trinity for all kinds or work in science, art, music or invention.

The formation of this trinity found in name or birth number shows the individual either has the power of creating, perfecting and expressing something for the betterment of mankind or should strive to attain it.

No. 2, being the center, means it should gather and collect for the use of the whole trinity, rather than for the individual self.

The highest use of a life working in the 2 form is to collect and gather everything relating to the 1 and arrange it in a tabulated and systematic manner.

He is fitted as is no other number to draw out the greatness of others.

In this way he himself grows great in strength and wins golden honors as his reward.

His mineral, as well as his color, is gold.

Living between the 1 and 3 he should live a beautiful,

sheltered life. He is their helper and they should protect him as his system or composition, gold, is not fitted for rough work.

No. 2 should use as many gold objects and ornaments as possible and use the color in combinations.

No. 3

No. 3 separated from 1 and 2 is like a ship without a rudder, drifting over any water and expressing whatever color the forces around present.

Unless their true source is found theirs is an aimless life.

In order to think logically a person with a No. 3 birth path must have among his substances, found in his name, month, day or year, the digit of 1, 2, 3, or 8, 9, 11.

Or 4 or 6 will in a measure supply the materials necessary for a sequence of action. 11 is an exalted one, objective as well as subjective.

If a No. 3 possesses none of these numbers he should associate with himself persons using forces 1 and 2 and trust to their judgment. No. 3 expressing the combined effort of the three, as this is the mission of a good 3.

No. 1 creates, No 2 collects and No. 3 expresses, making a chain strong and beautiful which the world could ill spare.

This trinity expresses action of both body and mind. No. 3 should express all the characteristics of 1 and 2 and realize that it is the expression number of a golden trinity of concentrated action.

Its color is a flame of gold.

No. 4

No. 4, joined to No. 3, makes a discordant note.

A person using No. 3 force and living at his highest in union with his trinity of 1, 2, 3, finds a No. 4 note or color different to adjust to his consciousness.

A No. 3 person sees a project form its beginning, when the flame first emerges as 1, grows and blossoms through 2 and gains complete expression in 3.

A No. 4 person sees things on a level with his eyes. Everything, to him, is either useful or the reverse.

No. 4 looks at things from the individual standpoint and often fails to realize the Unity of the Whole.

When the soul rises to a higher level of consciousness the beauty of the No. 4 character shines forth grand and mighty, using words and acts that are strong and powerful, but always for individual, family or friends rather then for the race.

Their desire is always for full expression as shown by the vowels of the word four, which makes 4, the highest expression number.

No. 5

No. 5 individuals are exactly opposite in their nature to 4, differing widely in action and thought.

The world knows what to expect of those working in the 4 force of life, but with No. 5 the unexpected is always happening.

The substances found in the 5th vibration are totally different from those found in the 4th.

Life to a 5, is always interesting even though they weary of the many changes experienced.

The 5 force is the unseen force known as life.

When the Son of God, known as Jesus, walked the earth, he showed the highest of seen forms; He was individualized spirit vibrating in the highest of vibrations, the 11.

When He began His work as the Christ, and was known as such, His vibration dropped to 5, as this is a vibration that every soul on any plane can grasp and understand.

No. 5 pathway is filled with everything, both high and low, to be found in the experiences of life. It very seldom shows the effects of age.

As the pendulum of life swings backward and forward, it is the tendency of all vibrations to return to the 5 path.

It has the mystical possibilities perhaps not yet fully understood, just as no man fully understands what "life" means, which vibrates 5.

No. 6

No. 6 stands for the Cosmic Mother and holds desires as a mother holds her child.

This number will aid the person having it, to give free expression to his soul if he will hold to the unity of his life and keep the flame of spirit burning in order that the children of men may see the light and know where to walk.

No. 7

This number holds the memories of the Earth currents and shows by its expression that it realizes the limitations of the children of men and their fullness.

No. 8

No. 8 is the beginning of another cycle, one outside of the regular routine of life.

In this pathway are found substances (material things which vibrate 8) fashioned and worked out by Nos. 4, 5, 6 and 7.

The path of the 8 is strewn with the unsatisfactory attempts made by others.

It is the duty and pleasure of No. 8 to look them over, set them up, and with a chisel carve them into forms which will benefit the ones who, in an immature way, have previously struggled with them.

The sound of their tools resound in harmony with C, the musical note of Creation. This fundamental C rings out, clear and high, from all created things, sending out a flame of canary, the color composed of the gold of 2, the green of 4, with a tinge of the scarlet of the 6 vibration.

From these materials 8 builds structures for the race, but it takes the vigor of 9 to give them full expression.

In this trinity of 8, 9, 11, the same is manifested as in 1, 2, 3, but on a higher plane.

The first trinity of mind, so its action is more or less concrete.

The last trinity, 8, 9, 11, is the trinity of spirit, so its action is universal.

The weakness of this trinity lies in its indifference to conventional standards of thought and action.

This applies equally to 8, 9, 11, 22.

Because they have outgrown certain standards they should not be heedless of their more backward brethren whom those aids are intended to help.

No. 9

No. 9 is composed of all the numbers, but especially of 3 and 6.

It is the highest vehicle of expression and holds within itself all the possibilities of the first trinity.

But it is no longer a flame of gold, burning with a steady light; it has added the blood of all nations and tribes, and endeavors to express the feelings of every phase of humanity, always entertaining, at the same time, a feeling of comradeship, even for the lowest.

When 9 realizes that his color, red, represents the blood of all mankind, is the vital color of life and that he must express all things and all phases of life without himself going into the mire, he will find a joy in life not to be found outside of the 9 vibration.

This is what Red means.

With the 9 vibration the paths of life, according to Pythagoras, end.

No. 11 and 22

The Ancients believed and taught that a mystical meaning attached to numbers and there was much esoteric meaning concealed in the arrangement of the Hebrew alphabet.

It was composed of 22 letters; the highest point was reached in 11, while the fundamental letters were 1 and 22.

They taught that 1 was the beginning; the height was reached in 11 and collected in 22.

No. 11

There is in the world a class of people no man can understand, nor do they often understand themselves. These people vibrate in name 11 or 22. They may be found in every pathway of life, giants of strength, upon all planes, and yet at times, when judged by the intellect, correspondingly weak.

No 11 represents the highest type of everything found, whether on the mineral, vegetable or animal plane.

They are strong, gentle souls who, when they find it necessary to administer justice, become as inflexible as iron.

The reach the full octave of sound and color.

The can feel every note of everything both seen and unseen and yet many 11's are inactive or asleep, when if they would arouse themselves they could partake in all the exalted joys of the universe.

We never add 11 to make a digit. No man has a right to interfere with God's message.

No. 22

22 is a high, free 2 with its proclivities for collecting upon the higher planes into cooperation.

Its colors are all the colors and all the sounds to be in the Octave of D.

Like 11, No. 22 has left behind the mere material good of 2, which it has already lived through, perhaps, more than once, and now life is illumined with the glow from the ideal regions.

To live in 22 is more difficult than to live in one of the lower vibrations, but if the lower is chosen instead of a higher the joy is lost.

We never add 22, as they stand apart from the rest of the world, by the law of opposites, either stronger or weaker than the average man or woman.

Its color is cream, showing that it means to gather together all that seems good to its trinity of 8, 9, 11 or 22 and join them in cooperation with all the forms and colors.

To summarize the meaning of the numbers:

1 means Unity and Creation. Its color is flame. Its note, C.

2 means collecting and tabulating. Its color is gold. Its note, D.

3 means expressing 1 and 2. Its color is a gold flame. Note, E.

4 means physical and mental force. Its colors are blue and green. Note, F.

5 means Life and Sex. Its color is pink. Note, G.

6 means a Cosmic Mother. Its colors are scarlet, orange and heliotrope. Note, A.

7 means Earth, its joys and shadows. Its colors are purple, steel, brick and magenta. Note, B.

8 means Free forms. Resurrection. Its color is canary. Note, any C.

9 means Free expression on all planes. The Soul of things. Its color is red. Note, any D.

11 means Exaltation. The height of seen forms. Its colors are yellow and violet, white and black. Notes, whole octave of C–C.

22 means Cooperation. It color is cream. Notes, whole octave of D–D.

CHAPTER 2

The Mission of the Birth Force

Nature always works through the trinity of Substance, Force and Consciousness.

The first part consists of things seen, called matter; the second part is force or power; these two create the third part, called consciousness.

The birth numbers of month, day and year show the substances made active by the birth force which is found by taking the digit of month, day and year added together, while the name shows the kind of consciousness already attained.

For instance, and to make it plainer, a person is born with names vibrating 3, 11. This is their rate of consciousness. Their birth month is 3, day 1, year 2. 1 + 2 + 3 = 6. They are using the 6 force.

The 1, 2, 3 show the quality of substance. They must attack with their 6 force and be able to related them to their 3, 11 consciousness or if they use any other name they can relate them to its consciousness.

But if they had been born with a low name vibration and a high birth vibration, life would have presented more difficulty to them because they would not have had the quality of consciousness to understand what was needed.

No matter what your birth vibration is, your name will show how much of it you can understand.

Your name is your source of supply. As a stream cannot rise above its source, so an individual cannot go above the level of his consciousness; he will see everything from that standpoint.

If you do not like the conscious relation you bear to things in general, open your eyes, your brain, your heart and rise to a higher level of consciousness.

That is why are you on the earth. You are living in order to advance.

If a person has a No. 4 name or rate of consciousness and a No. 11 birth vibration, he will see life from the level of 4 until by growth he rises and seeks higher levels.

This growth can be made by living in, and in harmony with, one's own force as shown by the month, day, and year added to get the digit of birth, and by persistently dealing with the substances showing the same digits as the day, month and year taken separately.

Use the things to which your birth numbers are related, study them and learn the lessons they teach you.

To recapitulate to make it clear:

The digit of the numbers of month, day and year, taken separately, show the substances with which one should deal. Suppose, for instance, that one of your digits is 4. Then some of the substances especially related to you are silver, ochre, emerald, hemlock, coffee, strawberry, pineapple. If another part should be 6, you can include poplar, palm, orange, quince, crescent, laurel, japonica, topaz, diamond and borax.

In this way find out the substances positively related to you.

Then to know what kind of power you possess with which to use these substances, add together the separate digits of month, day and year and the digit of the whole will give your force.

For instance, say you were born April 24, 1885.

April is month 4, day 24, gives digit 6, and 1885 added together gives a digit of 22. Now we never add 22, so the force available is 4 + 6 = 10 or 1 and 22.

Your birth force is 1, 22.

It is to be hoped that the person so born has a high vibrating name or he will not be able to understand his birth force.

But if he was born with a name vibrating 4, 5, 6, or 7 and this birth path of 1, 22 he can by persistent effort eventually reach to the level of consciousness necessary to understand its meaning.

This was his object in coming into earth life. This was the task he set himself to do. In order to advance we can be greatly helped by a judicious use of color.

Perhaps there is no subject so misunderstood as reincarnation. Even thinking minds relate it to transmigration, which is entirely different. The soul of every man is a part of God who, for unknown reasons to us, sought through life's journeys to become perfect, as the Son of God is perfect. Since Creation's dawn it has always been clothed in the image of God. Ever since Creation ceased, at the Seventh period, it has been somewhere–some place–in the place God chose for it upon some plane of thought or action manifesting in the mystical substance its soul called for its use and best suited to the plane upon which it existed. Science teaches we change every particle of bone, muscle and flesh within the period of 11 months.

If this is true we have reincarnated at least once a year from the time of our inhabiting the infant body our soul first called to its aid when desiring to cross the span of life, calling to it atoms that were attuned to the vibration in which it should pass thru this span of life found in its birth number. Our body, as a whole is striking the note of our birth force and is called our Life's Song. The song of this pause in life's journey.

When we recognize them to the limit of our knowledge, we will have fulfilled the Physical Law, that of the body plane. When we have fulfilled the law of the earth plane to the fullest extent of our knowledge, we may trust God to erect upon the physical structure we have reared a perfect and harmonious adjustment of body, soul and spirit; so that we may be always certain that anything which enters our environment is sent by the Highest.

We do not need to question nor do anything but accept whatever we find confronting us. Hold the thing as the hand of a friend, for no matter how it appears, the Father sent it or it could not have entered our environment where Truth reigns.

The Cosmic Law speaks and acts through different expressions of the One Force according to the strength of its vibration, moving at its appropriate rate of speed. Moving at a certain rate it has sound, at another rate color.

The questions are constantly asked–

How can we tell where we belong?

What especial work should we do in order to advance?

Who chose our place and condition here?

These questions we shall endeavor to answer.

The digit of the name we use shows what we are at the time we use the name. That is, the name shows the rate of consciousness. It shows how much you can understand.

So the name may stand as the record of the work you have done in past lives, or states of consciousness somewhere.

The digit of your birth path will tell you the part you came to fill in this life. This number shows the work you have to do.

Your own spiritual part chose this path in order to give you the experiences needed to develop your weak points.

It seems probable that where a person's name number is repeated in his birth digit that in his past station he did not learn his lesson well and he has come back to do his imperfect work over again.

We should especially love and cherish our birth colors which we chose when we saw with the true vision of the Spirit and when we knew what was necessary for our perfect development.

The separate digits of month, day and year show the various substances which are positively related to you, and the numbers added together and the digit found will give the force you have at your command with which to attack these substances.

The name can be changed and will be as soon as you have really made an advance through the experiences to be found in your birth force. But the same birth force must be used all through this span of life; you grow by advancing its quality.

The vowels of your name, which show the hidden desire of your soul, will generally be found embodied in the birth path, in this way ultimately enabling you to attain your desire.

When it is once attained you will make some change in your name to show the growth, or add a degree of some kind.

The soul, clothed in flesh, has its own rate and quality of force. It may be working at a high rate, but it will only be conscious of its strength according to its own rate of consciousness as shown by the name.

The name records the growth of the soul.

The birth force shows the special work the soul came to do.

The vibration of each individual differs with the vibration of the things he is related to and the quality of force he is using during this span of life.

This birth force is his instrument for use during all this life's journey.

When we were ready to come into this world, with the sure knowledge of Spirit, we chose the path in life which contained the many experiences necessary to strengthen our weak points and advance the growth of the soul, in order to make what is called character.

The digit of the birth path shows the kind of work we need to do–its quality, color and sound or musical note.

So if we are doing the work we came to do, we know just which force we are using.

Through this work we grow into higher relationship of consciousness.

When a growth is actually made it will show in a change in our name number, which will take a higher vibration or become more harmonious.

Everything in the universe is an expression of spiritual strength. The expression may be faulty, for the instrument may not be properly attuned, but the principle never fails. It is as true and as easy to understand as the science of mathematics.

Besides color there is another factor to be taken into consideration, that is–sound.

Through vibration comes motion, through motion comes color, through color comes tone.

Every living soul, even the humblest, is attuned to one certain note; advanced souls being attuned to a whole octave of sound. C is the first letter of the musical scale and that note corresponds to No. 1.

This makes D correspond to No. 2, E to No. 3, F to 4, G to 5, A to 6, B to 7, and 8 and 9 begin again with C and D.

11 expresses the whole octave of C, while 22 expresses the whole octave of d.

Thus

C D E F G A B

1 2 3 4 5 6 7

8 9

To understand the meaning of your birth force after you have found it, remember that

1 means Unity and Creation, and that its color is flame.

2 means collecting and its color is gold.

3 means expressing 1 and 2 and its color is a gold flame.

4 means mental and physical force and its colors are blue and green.

5 means Life and Sex. Its color is pink.

6 means a Cosmic Mother. Its colors are scarlet, orange and heliotrope.

7 means the fullness of the earth and the shadows thereof. Its colors are purple, steel and magenta.

8 means Resurrection. Free forms. Its color is canary.

9 means full expression on all planes. Its colors are yellow, violet, black, white.

11 means a priest, a messenger. Its colors are yellow, violet, black, white.

22 means Cooperation. Its color is cream.

Your aura is the force of your system of body, soul and spirit expressed in finer form and it speaks through color. It should extend thirty feet in all directions.

You can find the meaning and message of all colors, as well as of everything else in the seen and unseen world by finding its vibration.

For instance, 1 vibrates flame and is composed of the following substances:

F vibrates 6, a common mother.

L vibrates 3, an expression of creation.

A vibrates 1, an invisible creative flame.

M vibrates 4, physical and mental force.

E vibrates 5, life and sex.

= 19[2]

10[3] Unity

1[4] Unity

Unity is the keynote of flame and is the quality of its force.

---

[1] 6 + 3 + 1 + 4 + 5 = 19
[3] 1 + 9 = 10
[4] 1 + 0 = 1

When the flame of life burns with spiritual intent, it illumines without destroying.

When the negative action prevails, as in untrained animals, it becomes a destroyer instead of an illuminator.

Flame is a collection of mental and physical rays, held in unity for the illumination or the destruction of that with which it comes into contact. Its objective message is that it is a light when actuated by the spirit.

When the spirit is absent it is a destroyer.

Its internal message, shown by its vowels, is the mother principle which while it loves, chides, for the child's advancement.

It speaks of the Creative Force in every ray and is intended to aid in the advancement of the race.

No. 2

No. 2 vibrates gold, which color is composed of the following qualities of substances:

G – 7 speaks for the earth and its varied experiences.

O – 6 speaks of the protecting love of Mother Earth.

L – 3 speaks for the desire to express the collection of gold forces.

D – 4 speaks for its desire to use mental and physical force.

= 20[5]

2 Gold

---

[5] 7 + 6 + 3 + 4 = 20

Gold means a collection of forces used to move substances that vibrate 2. It is the color which calls the attention of the force of creation to the activities of earth and yet it is inactive except in gathering and collecting for the other part of itself, the 3, to express.

In 3 it appears as a gold flame and no longer as the dross of the mineral gold.

It is believed by some mystics that this is the only color impenetrable to lower, so-called evil forces.

But we know that when there is a perfect trinity of body, soul and spirit as 1, 2, 3 represents, that it must be an illumined gold.

No. 3

No. 3 should speak for the illumined flame of gold and express these characteristics, especially as this quality is repeated in the vowels of three which are 1, meaning a flame of gold. Nos. 1, 2, 3 should wear gold colors and use, when possible, gold instruments and ornaments.

No. 4

No. 4 vibrates blue and green, representing the bustle of the green earth and the silence of the blue firmament.

Blue vibrates the 4 force. Within this color of blue other voices speak, using this physical form of substances:

B vibrates 2, a collection of gold force.

L vibrates 3, an expression of gold force.

U vibrates 3, an expression of gold force.

E – vibrates 5, life and sex in pink tones.

= 13[6]

1 unity

3 expression

= 4[7]

Blue wishes you to know that it holds within its system, as its letters prove, a collection of substances of gold forces trying to express themselves, and also holds the pink ray made visible.

When light or dark is added to its vibration it rises and finds its level in higher consciousness.

It message is "Look into me deeply and you will find more of Heaven."

The esoteric message found in its vowels is: "I am life."

Green also vibrates to the force of 4 and is composed of :

G vibrates 7, earth and its experiences.

R vibrates 9, free expression.

E vibrates 5, life and sex.

E – vibrates 5, life and sex.

N – vibrates 5, life and sex.

---

[6] 2 + 3 + 3 + 5 = 13

[7] 1 + 3 = 4

= 31[8]

3 expression

1 unity

= 4[9]

Green lacks the balanced sequence of 1, 2, 3 and is not a fully harmonious vibration. It hold the forces of earth together with deep purple and steel and pink repeated over and over.

It brings the message of silver and greenbacks to be gained by effort.

This is the objective message of green, but its esoteric message, as shown by its vowels, is that you must unite yourself in mind with the One God.

The 1 shows it to be a flame and the 2 is bound up in the mental and physical force of the 4. This makes green burn with a blue and green light. But 2 is in bondage.

No doubt the reason 13 is considered an unlucky number is from the lack of sequence 1, 2, 3.

Green shows this lack of perfection in her constant decay; but 1 and 3 give a power of expression which is always repeating itself.

The world loves green; its vibration is low and can be reached by anyone without effort either conscious or unconscious.

When light or dark is added, spiritual strength is given it.

---

[8] 7 + 9 + 5 + 5 + 5 = 31

[9] 3 + 1 = 4

No. 5

No. 5 pink and is composed of the following substances:

P vibrates 7 the earth and all it contains.

I vibrates 9, complete expression.

N vibrates 5, life and sex.

K vibrates 2, a collection of gold.

= 23[10] Gold

2

3

= 5[11] Life and sex

This, also, is not a perfect color, as the substances composing it show by their vibration, resolving themselves into 2, 3. This is a part of the first trinity. In green 2 was lacking' in pink it is the omission of 1, the creative power.

Pink is not a flame; it is an effort of life to rise to higher expression. It shows collection and expression, but lacks unity.

Many authorities condemn pink as a color and it is this lack of full strength they unconsciously feel.

It is a combination of red and gold, so filled with the spiritual white as to appear weak to eyes which judge the imperfect efforts of life as worthless.

Life, love and home vibrate to this spiritual imperfect pink.

Its objective message is: "I am a collection of everything in life, love and home, longing to express the soul of all

---

[10] 7 + 9 + 5 + 2 = 23

[11] 2 + 3 = 5

things. I am changeable, but always fascinating."

Its esoteric message is stronger than its objective force, as it is a call for full expression of soul and human brotherhood.

No. 6

Orange, scarlet and heliotrope all use the 6 rate of force, but express it in different ways.

Six lies in the heart of the free eleven, but its colors are not truly free. They lie in the heart of freedom and long for full expression, as is shown by the vowel of six, 9.

O vibrates 6, and means a Cosmic mother.

R vibrates 9, complete expression.

A vibrates 1, unity and creation.

N vibrates 5, life and sex.

G vibrates 7, earth with its remembrances.

E vibrates 5, life and sex.

= 33[12]

3

3

= 6[13]

Orange is a Cosmic mother who hold your wishes as a mother holds her child. She will aid you in giving expression if you will hold to unity and keep your flame burning in order to give light to the children of its esoteric message, found in the vowels, is to hold in unity life's expression.

---

12 6 + 9 + 1 + 5 + 7 + 5 = 33

13 3 + 3 = 6

Scarlet:

S vibrates 1, unity and creation.

C vibrates 3, complete expression.

A vibrates 1, unity and creation.

R vibrates 9, free expression.

L vibrates 3, expression.

E vibrates 5, life and sex.

T vibrates 2, collection.

= 24[14]

A collection of mental and physical forces held in the breast of the cosmos.

The message scarlet brings is this: "If you will hold to the unity of your life, create and express what lies under your hand for the advancement of others and your own higher self; I will aid you in health and in all things requiring fostering care."

Its esoteric message is the same as the objective.

Scarlet is one of the voices of the universe speaking to you.

Heliotrope:

H vibrates 8, free forms, or resurrection.

E vibrates 5, life and sex.

L vibrates 3, expression.

I vibrates 9, soul expression.

O vibrates 6, a cosmic mother.

---

[14] **1 + 3 + 1 + 9 + 3 + 5 + 2 = 24**

T vibrates 2, collection.

R vibrates 9, soul expression.

O vibrates 6, a cosmic mother.

P vibrates 7, the earth and its fullness.

E vibrates 5, life and sex.

= 60[15]

6

0

= 6, a cosmic mother

Heliotrope brings you a message from the plane above the normal gamut of vision. It is filled with prophetic voices and sees and knows without the aid of reason.

Its esoteric message is found in the voice of 4. The intellect must guide on this plane, to keep from physical destruction.

No. 7

One of the mixed colors of 7 is purple.

P vibrates 7, the earth and its experiences.

U vibrates 3, expression.

R vibrates 9, soul expression.

P vibrates 7, the earth.

L vibrates 3, expression

E vibrates 5, life and sex.

= 34[16]

3

4

= 7[17]

---

[15] 8 + 5 + 3 + 9 + 6 + 2 + 9 + 6 + 7 + 5 = 60

[16] 7 + 3 + 9 + 7 + 3 + 5 = 34 [17] 3 + 4 = 7

3 and 4, as found in the purple force, are discordant notes.

Treading the wine press alone, while the rich purple juices flow forth, by "pressure from above," purple brings you its refined and beautiful message, holding all life's joys and pains within its system. From it you can select any thought or action desired and in a limited way it will be your helper.

Its esoteric message is higher than it objective form. At center it is a radiant canary, asking you who are working in the purple force to rise to a free resurrected life, dropping earth's shadows to enter the shining yellow light.

A cosmic mother means a man or woman, is not related to sex.

No. 8

8 Speaks in the voice through substance of canary:

C vibrates 3, expression.

A vibrates 1, unity, creation.

N vibrates 5, life and sex.

A vibrates 1, unity

R vibrates 9, soul expression

Y vibrates 7 and its experiences.

= 26[18]

2

6

= 8[19], freedom and resurrection.

---

[18] 3 + 1 + 5 + 1 + 9 + 7 = 26

[19] 2 + 6 = 8

The color, canary, represents the free 8 vibration and holds within its system the gold of 2, the green of and a touch of scarlet from 6. All of these are mingled together in unity, like the blood of different races.

This color is found in many of the semi-precious stones as well as in the Opal, which is the messenger of canary.

This color is found in Fire, Earth, Air, and Water and is a messenger from all realms.

It holds a deep gold center as its esoteric message.

No. 9

Red and Brown.

R vibrates 9, free expression of the soul.

E vibrates 5, life and sex.

D vibrates 4, mental and physical force.

= 18[20]

1

8

= 9[21], free expression of soul.

Red brings you the message of complete expression, from the wail of the condemned criminal to the anthems of those who have never known sin.

It changes in negative or positive action from love to hate, either of which it can express with equal vigor.

It deals with life on all planes and with all kinds of love.

---

[20] 9 + 5 + 4 = 18

[21] 1 + 8 = 9

It attracts the same as it brings, as it contains all mental and physical force from 1 to 9.

Love and use this color, but realize both its weakness and its strength.

Its esoteric message is for free expression of life and sex.

Brown.

B vibrates 2, collection.

R vibrates 9, free expression.

O vibrates 6, a cosmic mother.

W vibrates 5, life and sex.

N vibrates 5, life and sex.

= 27[22]

2, collects.

7, a cosmic mother.

= 9[23], freedom and resurrection.

Brown brings you a more negative message than red. The more gold a thing contains the less it expresses unless it is a luminous gold, in which you may act, but the tendency of the ordinary brown shade is inactivity.

The darker or lighter the shade, the more action it contains.

To escape earth's shadow it should possess a texture. Its esoteric message is to hold, as a mother does, her family in the unity of the whole.

---

22 2 + 9 + 6 + 5 +5 = 27

23 2 + 7 = 9

No. 11

Black, White, Yellow and Violet.

The message of black is:

B vibrates 2, a collection of yellow force.

L vibrates 3, expression of 1 and 2.

A vibrates 1, unity, creation.

C vibrates 3, expression

K vibrates 2, collection

= 11[24]

Black contains the sequence of thought and action found in 1, 2, 3. It begins and ends with 2, thus binding the color outwardly in negative form. It absorbs instead of reflecting. Its esoteric message is a flame of all colors, longing to emerge.

White brings the message of life. It begins and ends with life vibration exalted to the highest form as is shown by the complete spiritual trinity, 8, 9, 11.

It contains and expresses all colors, all thoughts, all tones, all actions; in short, it is a perfect expression of everything from the highest to the lowest. Its esoteric voice speaks for full expression.

Yellow.

---

[24] 2 + 3 + 1 + 3 +2 = 11

Y vibrates 7, earth experiences.

E vibrates 5, life and sex.

L vibrates 3, expression.

L vibrates 3, expression

O vibrates 6, collection

W vibrates 5, life and sex.

= 29[25]

2

9

= 11[26]

Yellow begins with earth and ends with free life.

It contains the consciousness of highest sight seeing and hearing. When negative it may express jealousy and hate. When positive it contains all creation, helping and assisting everything to climb the universal heights.

Its esoteric message is the same as its outer form, making it a color of undiminished glory and strength.

Violet.

V vibrates 4, mental and physical force.

I vibrates 9, full soul expression.

O vibrates 6, a cosmic mother.

L vibrates 3, expression

E vibrates 5, life and sex.

T vibrates 2, a collection.

= 29[27]

---

[25] 7 + 5 + 3 + 3 + 6 + 5 = 29

[26] 2 + 9 = 11

2

9 A complete trinity is found in 2, 9, 11.

= 11[28]

Violet tells of having gained complete soul expression in an upper realm. When positive it contains the strength and energy of the masculine. It center shows a collection of gold forces, maternal in feeling and expression.

No. 22

Cream.

C vibrates 3, expression.

R vibrates 9, soul expression.

E vibrates 5, life and sex.

A vibrates 1, unity and creation.

M vibrates 4, mental and physical force.

= 22[29]

22 is 11 times stronger than 2 but possesses many of its qualities. It gathers together all the other vibrations and leads them into cooperation.

It is not a fundamental color. It has no individuality. All its strength lies in cooperation.

At its center it is holding up the torch of life.

If 22 should be the digit of one of your names, it shows

---

27 4 + 9 + 6 + 3 + 5 + 2 = 29

28 2 + 9 = 11

29 3 + 9 + 5 + 1 + 4 = 22

that one part of your nature has reached the 22 consciousness, and this part will aid the rest to rise into the cream light.

If 22 is part of your birth vibration, it will help the other parts to grow into conscious relation with it.

When a name shows no higher vibration than 7, in separate parts of the digit of the whole, the owner of such names is conscious of its color, form and manner of growth. He knows where it should be planted to give the best effect. It is to him merely a flower belonging to the vegetable kingdom. The study of Botany is satisfying to such a person as is his knowledge of the habits of the flower.

The owner of a name composed of various digits whose sum when added makes 8, 9, 11 or 22, will look at the same flower and note its color, form and odor, becoming especially conscious, as he approaches it of its aura made known by its perfume.

He looks upon the little flower as part of the whole order of creation; he speaks to it as to a friend; he lifts up its broken stalk as he would the wing of a bird and when it finds place upon his person he regards it as a thing occupying its own place in the universe with himself.

When these people hear music they may be careless as to the name of the composer or of the instruments used.

It seems as if they had once dwelt where music had had a power over them and that power had fled. They now hear it as a part of the whole and the whispering of the leaves in the forest or the warbling of a bird's song will recall or set into motion a whole gamut of sound for their inner ear which will satisfy them.

To those whose consciousness has not passed the limit of 7, all the technique of music is studied and used. They know all about the composer's style, they dissect every piece, criticize and admire its parts and delight in its execution.

We find most band leaders vibrating 6, 5 or 3.

Theodore Thomas is an exception, as he vibrates in consciousness to 5, 22, which means life in cooperation.

If your level of consciousness does not satisfy you as revealed by your name, grow into a higher relation which will cause you to change your name.

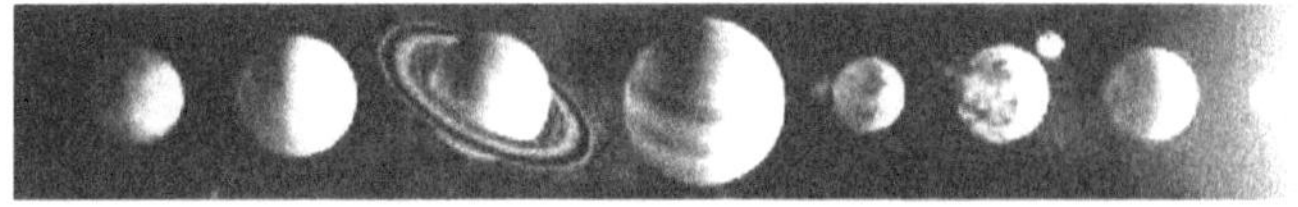

CHAPTER 3

Cosmic Adjustment

Have there not been days in your life when certain thoughts possessed you which you desired to put into action? When you resolved on the morrow, or some other certain day to give them expression? But when the time fixed upon arrived you found that the desire which had actuated you had vanished with the day that gave it birth. We usually say, "After sleeping on it I changed my mind."

But the change was not caused by sleep; it lay deeper. The cause lay in the unseen forces dominating the universe.

In all nature no two things can be found exactly alike; no two days are ever the same.

As the earth constantly changes its position in regard to the sun, causing changes of season, changes of temperature and setting into action different forces with each day, so each day has its own special vibration which affects certain substances (by this word I mean all seen things) which are vibrating at the same rate.

To find the rate of vibration of any substance add together the number of the letters which compose its name, then find the digit of the numbers. This will tell the rate of vibration, which is its force.

Nature always acts through Substance, Force and Consciousness. The action of substance and force create the third part, called consciousness.

If you wish to know how you are related to the earth and spirit planes you can make all things speak to you through color and sound as found by the scientific basis of Number Vibration.

The force or energy which dominates a day is of the quality and strength of the force that is loosened by the position of the earth to the sun; this gives the color which disclosed its rate of vibration.

The blue mists always hover over the Alleghenies[30] forming so dense a color that the ordinary eye can see and comprehend it. Yet behind and beneath this constant color there is always another color which changes with each succeeding day in accord with Nature's Law.

When we are clothed in harmony with the day we are one with the cosmic force of the day, and become an active force, something to be counted with, instead of being an obstacle or one of the things merely acted upon.

---

[30] the western part of the Appalachian Mountains; extending from northern Pennsylvania to southwestern Virginia, in the United States of America.

In selecting a wardrobe, thought should be given to prepare garments of various colors so as to have them ready to use upon the days when earth and air are enveloped in the same colors.

Wear the colors belonging to the day and you and they will frolic in the cosmic harmony; they will speak for your success in love and business.

Find the vibration of each day and the color belonging to it by adding together the day, month and year and then finding the digit, unless again either day or month should be 11 or 22. In that case find the digit of the remaining number. For example, take November 22, 1910. Here November is 11, which must be kept separate; 22 is the same, and the digit of 1910 is 11. So November 22, 19110, would 11, 22, 11, a double force of 1 1, together with 22.

A normal physical body is attuned to the force of cosmic energy expressed by its birth number as shown by the digit of the day, month and year in which it came to earth life.

Your body is made of this vibratory force, or to make it plainer, the atoms of your body should vibrate to the force dominating the substances showing the same vibration.

You own individual force should be made to harmonize with each day's force in order that all the forces about you may become your loving helpers.

If you have more than one color in your birth digit, use the one which harmonizes with the force of the day. Should you have but one color, as gold, which expresses the first trinity, 1, 2, 3, and the vibration of the day is pink, use the gold, as pink is composed of yellow, red and white, or else us a salmon pink. If our name reveals a pink vibration in its concord, use that.

Should your force of gold and the Queen of the Day be riding in her chariot of blue or green and you have neither a blue or green vibration, remember that this is not a good day for you to inaugurate activities.

When possible spend it in reading or meditation in order to store up knowledge to be used at a time when Nature is more conscious of your presence.

Seven gowns or less will serve to clothe you in cosmic harmony; or you can use a variety of scarfs or veils.

The force of the day is Spirit, or at least it has spirit quality. When it touches the earth it vitalizes the substances the sun is acting upon.

When different forces are in harmony there is a perfect carnival of joyousness. Is it not then wiser to join in the frolic rather than to let it pass by on the other side?

We must always do our part in life before we can expect help from the Divine. What man can do to help himself the Father will never do. But when one has struggled to the limit of his powers in quest of health, of light or holy consciousness, the Father then stretches forth his hand and opens a door to fresh power. This will not be done until the Law upon the physical plane has been observed.

Honest souls often wonder why the law of abundance is not set in action for their benefit, when they themselves are the obstacles, they not having fulfilled the physical law, which is the foundation upon which the higher laws must act to supply human needs.

For instance, if one spends a quarter for a cigar, while he owes the quarter to someone else, he, by the act, enters the vibration of the person to whom he is indebted, becomes his servant, as it were, loses the strength of his own life force and closes the vibration of abundance. Later, when the law of equity has been complied with, possible that fasting and prayer may once more free his own forces, and when they are loosened, all the forces of nature will help that man dip deep into the realm of abundance.

Certain fixed laws upon the sense plane must be met and no amount of mental effort will restore a broken physical law.

To be entirely happy in this world, one must have a balanced body, soul and spirit. To err against any of these parts is to commit an equal sin which tells the story in broken health and poverty of thought and material substances.

One cannot afford to sleep through this stage of activity. We came to earth to work and win experience upon all planes of life.

The age when the higher consciousness of a person awakens is of little consequence in regard to results. Simply begin.

It has been proven to the satisfaction of many that none of the foods that aid in building the body of man come from the earth.

Plants and minerals serve simply as means to attract substances from the upper realm or the plane beyond sight.

The atmosphere contains everything man needs. At the present time man's level of consciousness is not high enough to maintain a true balance; therefore, in his imperfect state, as he cannot take in his food from the air, he must eat and drink.

There is a science called "Celestial Chemistry," by means of which we may gather in "Bread from Heaven." We shall have to do this until our race advances sufficiently to know that our real support come from the plane beyond sight.

Colors are an important aid in our advancement. One color gathers carbon food, and other colors their own kind.

The sun, whose vibration, 9, shows it to be a full, free expression, is the Great Alchemist set apart to work in the activities of the spheres as man's helper while on this plane of action.

Everyone should aid Nature by replacing his worn out tissues by those of health structure. To do this call to your aid your birth force, which will always prove to be your true friend.

The quality of this force is found by finding the digit of the day, month and year of your birth, and this is your instrument for use during all this span of life. Unless your own force finds points of contract with the Cosmic force, it is obliged to lie dormant in an inactive body.

One way to aid Nature is to have colored glass boxes or jars made dust proof, into which water or certain food can be put which you wish to vitalize.

Allow them to remain in the sun's rays for half a day or less. The substance or food will then be replete with the iron or other quality the color of the glass has called into action. One should have jars of the primary colors, red, blue and yellow, as the intermediate colors can be made by blending these three colors.

These three colors, blue, red and yellow, represent the vibrations 4, 9, 11. The 11 vibrates yellow, the 9 red and the 4 blue.

The sun, the great Celestial Chemist, supplies oxygen in the air as food, but we, to do our part, must breathe it in deep, so the food may reach every cell, for cells are furnaces where heat is made.

We know that when we join an acid and an alkali in proper proportions we generate a power which scientists call electrical. We know that every part of flesh is filled with tiny cells to hold the acids and the alkalies in order to generate physical power. We know that when the acids and alkalies in man are present in proper proportion he has a strong physique.

Then we also know that while the system is in balance containing just enough acids and just enough alkalies, there is no weakness or disease.

If there is a lack of alkali the man is sour.

For a Test

Get from a druggist a piece of litmus paper and dampen it with saliva. If the saliva is acid the paper will turn red. If it does not turn, and you are not in normal health, the alkalies are in excess.

Saliva in its normal state is slightly alkaline.

When acids are in great excess, refrain from eating acid fruit and other food which causes an acid fermentation when they meet the gastric juice, which in its normal state is also acid.

The question of fasting–of how and when to do it–is one of the vital questions of the day. Here is one of Nature's formulas. When one is weak because the acids and the alkalies are not properly balanced, refrain from eating anything for 60 hours, after which for seven days eat only once a day sparingly and of the simplest food.

Flush the bowels frequently and drink a glass of water every waking hour.

Sleep out of doors or with your window open–let every breathe be deep and full and let the thought of cleansing follow well the breath trying by thought to throw the finer ethers that you breathe to all parts of the body. This prescription, if followed, will turn weakness into strength.

The sun will help to gather from the upper realm the positive food we need to maintain a perfect physique if we will only give it the proper aid.

The excitants used in medicine are all red. We could mention Balsam of Peru, Iron, Musk, Cloves, Capsicum, Alcohol, and a host of others. Conditions which require red are those of collapse, when the blood is impoverished and stimulation is required. Then everything shows coldness, paleness, with a bluish color.

Red being the true arterial stimulant, it should not be used when plethora or inflammation is present.

When in need of red, place food and water in red jars, where the sun's rays can reach them and the sun will supply everything necessary for the debilitated man's well being.

The red rays appropriate a lot of phosphate which we need to give strength of blood, brain and brawn. In this way we can ironize the water we drink and fill it full of Nature's iron which will not overcharge parts of the body, as the mineral often does.

When body is weak because of impoverished blood, red garments will greatly aid. Putting on a red robe, with nothing under it, for forty or fifty minutes twice a day will help restore balance.

When blue is lacking in the system, use blue jars and a blue robe, the same as described for red.

Blue is an intellectual color as well as a physical one.

Blue is a nerve sedative.

Blue is cooling and astringent and will control inflammatory conditions.

When doctors wish to find a drug to do this kind of work, they seek a plant which bears a blue flower like aconite, belladonna, nitric acid and chloroform.

These drugs appear to help and sometimes do, because the force of the blue is brought into direct touch with the abnormal state. It may be taken direct from the sun in the food or drink.

The blue sun bath in the blue robe is excellent.

Yellow may be secured in the same way as red or blue by using yellow glasses and a yellow robe. This color is the great relaxant. It does the work which all cathartic remedies do.

Such remedies are made from the yellow force, such as sulphur, figs, castor oil, senna, colocynth, saffron, ginger, and podophyllum.

Drink water and eat food potentized by yellow rays of light or take the yellow sun bath in a robe made of the material called for by the birth force.

For example, one having 6 for his birth number should

use yellow silk, as 6 vibrates silk. A person having a birth force 1, 2, 3 will find a fine quality of wool health-giving, as it is the same vibration as the birth force.

When we transgress one of Nature's laws, we sin; and laws of Nature are the only ones we find upon the statute book of God.

Our body is not our own but is a part of Nature's Plan. It may be a very small and apparently unimportant part, but it belongs with the whole and any transgression against it will have to be answered for.

To sin against ourselves is to sin against the race, and to sin against all manifestation in Heaven and Earth.

The Universe is a unit and we are a part of the whole.

We may also sin against the world beneath us when we eat a perfect salad leaf without a thought of gratitude, or when we inhale the fragrance of the rose without realizing that we have entered and absorbed the aura of one of Nature's products.

When we advance to a feeling of gratitude to the worlds beneath us, which minister to our pleasure, our bodies will grow stronger and we will manifest keenness of appetite instead of dyspepsia.

When a disease manifests, finds its vibration–the outer form will be shown by the letters comprising the name and its hidden desire will be found in the vowels of the word. Then seek for the lack of balance and so of health.

The Spiritual Trinity, 8, 9, 11, holds the first trinity within its concord–2 is in 8; 3 is in 9; and 1 is in 11.

These foods will be moved or vitalized on any day with digit of **1**–Fried Oysters, Lamb, Codfish, Hot Cakes, Eggs, Lobster.

2 vibrates–Eggs, Shellfish.

3 vibrates–Meat, Steaks, Toast, Wine, Jelly, Clams, Potatoes, Cabbage, Hominy, Bread, Fruits, Cakes, Liquor, Beer, Milk Toast.

These three vibrations belong together and are in harmony.

4 vibrates–Oysters, Farinaceous food, Coffee, Veal, Cup Custard, Onion, Parsnips, Macaroni, Stew.

5 vibrates–Shad, Custard, Tobacco, Butter, Pastry, Baked Apples, Corned Beef, Beans, Lettuce.

6 vibrates–Orange, Bread Pudding, Mushrooms, Beets, Potatoes, Currants, Pork, Soft Boiled Eggs, Fish, Wine.

7 vibrates–Poached Eggs, Creamed Potatoes, Stewed Fruits, Spinach, Vegetable Soup, Crabs.

8 vibrates–Rice, Chicken, Barley Soup, Tea, Rice, Bacon, Games, Cauliflower, Vegetables, Shellfish, Soup, Stewed Oysters, Ice Cream.

9 vibrates–Milk Toast, Beef, Turnips, Milk, Cheese, Cup Custard, Raw Clams, Tomatoes, Desserts, Baked Potatoes, Oatmeal, Sago Pudding.

11 vibrates–Soft Boiled Eggs, Baked Apples, Clam, Drink.

22 vibrates–Cream Toast, Stewed Chicken, Water, Fruits, Ice Cream.

Vibrations **8, 9, 11** and **22** are in harmony.

Phosphate of Lime vibrates 6, its vowels equal 5–5/6. This remedy used for creating harmony in the bony structure acts through the red color, or scarlet, and pink upon food or liquids of any kind vibrating to the two other colors of yellow and blue. Anything vibrating to 4 or 11 will make a perfect trinity of colors which will act upon the bony structure of the body. Subject substances of 4, 11 vibration to the sun's rays or rays of light in closed in jars or boxes of red glass from 3 to 4 hours according to the sun's intensity when the enclosed substances will attract from the air and sun, a compound called albumen. This is a substance chemists have failed to analyze.

Find a few of the many substances vibrating to 4, 11, some of which are Oysters, Farinaceous Food, Coffee, Veal, etc. Water and drink vibrate to 11. Find fruits and many other substances used in daily food by their vibration.

Silica vibrates 8 with the internal structure 1 = 8/1. This is called an element and shows a high vibration. It is a constitutional remedy and used to create resurrection of the body from the old to the new.

It acts upon bony structure and the skin. Use yellow light 4 hours, blue 15 minutes, upon substances vibrating 8 and 1, always water subjected to the same rays.

Fluoride of Lime vibrates objectively 6 and internally 7 + 6/7. It holds the body together and its effect can be replaced by using the food subjected to red rays 2 hours and blue and yellow rays 1 hour each.

Foods vibrating to 6 and 7 should be used. When this is lacking in the system every fiber is relaxed, all parts of the body sag, hacking cough is present, and the veins are swollen and diseased.

Phosphate of potash–1. Vowels 7. This remedy vibrates 1 and its vowels show a desire for 7 which means a unity of the body. It is used in nervous affections and gives activity to the brain. To get the same cure use yellow glass boxes, as 1 is yellow and subject food and drink to 3 hours' exposure and 1 hour each to red and blue rays. Use foods or substances vibrating 1 and 7.

Sulphate of soda vibrates 9 and has inward structure of 22 = 9/22. This is a strong vibration and governs the liquids of the body as the bile, the blood, etc.

It controls indigestion. Subject food and water to 2 hours red and 2 hours, yellow 2 hours, and blue 1/2 hour to get the cure of the remedy.

Phosphate of soda vibrates 6 internal structure 7 = 6/7. It is used to neutralize acids, to cure sour breath and all forms of acid diathesis. Subject foods and drinks vibrating 6 and 7 to 2 hours red, 1 hour yellow and 1 hour blue. Vitalize water the same as foods.

Rheumatism vibrates 1; its vowels are 9. The 9 contains the 3 quality, as it is 3 times 3, and 9 vibrates all shades of the prime red. 1 or 11 vibrates yellow. The blue color is missing in the trinity of colors and must be supplied by food vibrating 4; also water subjected 4 hours to blue rays.

Diabetes vibrates 11, its vowels equal 2. This disease lacks the balance of 3. Use food vibrating 9; also water subjected to 4 hours of red rays.

Tuberculosis vibrates 11, its spiritual structure found by its vowels is 9, making it two parts 11/9 the lacking part is the 8 or 1 quality of blue. Food vibrating 2, 4, and 8, also 22, exposed to blue rays 4 hours will supply the curative powers. Also drink an abundance of water vitalized by blue rays.

[31]**Hemorrhoids** vibrates 6, internal structure is 8, making 6/8. This disease needs the yellow light. Substances vibrating 1 and 11 exposed 4 hours to yellow light will supply the deficiency.

Scrofula vibrates 5, its internal structure 1, making 1/5. This shows a deficiency of the unity of life. It shows a pink yellow light and needs blue and red to give it balance. Expose food vibrating 4 and 9 to 3 hours blue rays and 1 red.

---

[31] I would refer the reader to a most excellent book called *"Principles of Light and Colors,"* by Babbit. The law of cure used in Nature's Symphony is according to the Balliet School of Philosophy of Numbers.

Dysentery vibrates 9, its vowels are of value 1, showing a lack of blue color. Use foods vibrating 4 and 8 exposed to blue rays 4 hours.

Hysteria vibrates 6, its vowels vibrate the same 6/6. The balance can be restored by using food exposed to 1 hour each of blue, red and yellow rays, using substances of 2, 4, 8, 3, 9 and 11.

Cramps vibrate 6, its internal structure is 1, making 6/1. This disease needs the blue and red rays. Subject food of 4, 3, 8 and 9 to 3 hours blue rays and 1 hour of red rays.

Constipation vibrates 11, its vowels are 4 = 11/4. This disease needs the balance of red. Use foods of 3, 6, 9 subjected to red rays 4 hours. Also water.

Debility vibrates 5 and its vowels are 5, making 5/5. This is a disease connected with sex life and must be cured by yellow and blue colors; also red, as the 5 vibrates pink. Stronger red rays are needed. Use food and drink subjected to 1 hour red rays, 2 hours to yellow, and 2 to blue. Use foods vibrating to 3, 9, 4 and 1.

Skin disease vibrates 7, its vowels 6. This disease is lacking the yellow rays. Subject substances and water vibrating 1 and 11 to 4 hours yellow rays.

Scalp vibrates 5, its vowels 1 = 1. It lacks the balance of 2. Subject food of 2 and 4 to 4 hours blue rays. Also use water subjected to blue rays.

Malaria vibrates 1, its vowels 3 = 1/3. It lacks the balance found in the blue rays. Use food vibrating 2 and 4. Also water will be found particularly curative, subject to 4 hours blue rays.

Anemia. The vowels equal 2 = 11/2. The missing element is 3 food vibrating 9. Also water exposed to red rays, 4 hours will supply the deficiency.

Scarlet Fever vibrates 6, 11, objectively, and the vowels are 6, 1. As scarlet is 6, both objectively, and the vowels are 6, 1, it holds and will not loosen. The disease lacks the blue rays foods vibrating 6, 11, 1, subjected to 4 hours blue rays. Also water will aid in the cure of the disease.

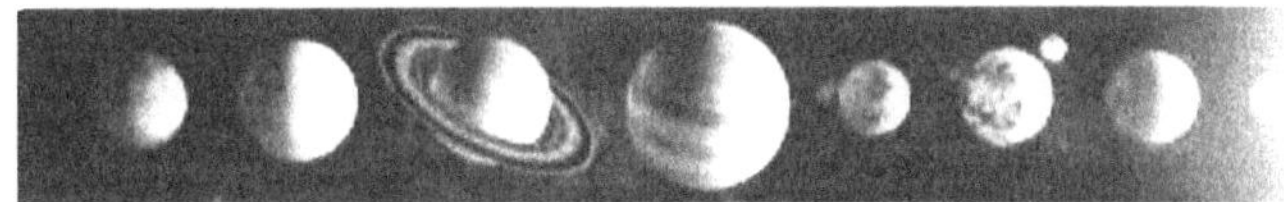

CHAPTER 4

Harmony in Dress

Have you noticed the different effect produced by different days, how on one day you desire to be constantly active, while on other days it is only by a great effort that anything is accomplished?

The cause of this lies in the unseen force dominating the Universe.

"In all nature no two things can be found exactly alike, no two days are ever the same."

Nature always acts through the Trinity of Substance, Force and Consciousness; the action of substance and force creating the third part called consciousness.

If you wish to find the rate of vibration of any substance, add together the numbers of the letters composing its name and find the digit. This will give the rate of vibration or the rate of force dominating the substance.

If we have vibration, we must have sound, if sound also color, and if any single thing failed to fulfill the law, chaos would result in the cosmos.

As the earth slowly changes its position in regard to the sun, one force after another becomes active, the one of today being held in abeyance until sometime in the future, when the same conditions will again call it into activity.

The Earth is always dressed in a garment of the color which speaks the will of the force which is active on that especial day. This force may be considered the Queen of the Day, and her reign is beneficent to those who are vibrating in harmony with the force she is expressing.

The force or energy which dominates a day is of the quality and strength of the force which is loosened by the position of the earth to the sun; this gives the color, which discloses its rate of vibration.

When we are clothed in harmony with the day we are one with the cosmic force of the day, and become an active force, something to be reckoned with, instead of being an obstacle or one of the things acted upon.

When the force of the day is yellow, it moves into action those things vibrating yellow light. Why should we, the highest development of nature on the earth, enrobe ourselves in discordant color, thereby standing aside in the shadows when we should be expressing harmony with the forces about us?

As the atoms of our body change constantly, we cannot afford to lose the delight of color harmony for even one day.

Most of our desires are connected in some way with substance; a desire to succeed with something that can be seen.

This thing called substance is strongly moved upon certain days by a color which may take either a positive or negative character.

Would it not then be wise, since most of our desires are connected with substance, and if we wish to get what we want, would it not be wise to clothe ourselves in harmonious colors and work with our forces and not against them?

When we do not work with them the forces of the day must work through the intellect alone, when the whole body should be frolicking in the glory of color.

When we are negative to a force its color may appear distasteful to us.

In selecting a wardrobe thought should be given to prepare garments of various colors so as to have them ready to use when earth and are enveloped in the same colors.

Wear the colors belonging to the day and they will frolic in the Cosmic Harmony. They will speak for your success in love and business.

A normal physical body is attuned to the force of energy expressed in its birth number, as shown by the digit of the month, day and year in which it came into earth life.

Your body is made of vibrating force, or to make it plainer, the atoms of your body should vibrate to the force dominating the substances showing the same vibration.

Your own individual force should be made to harmonize with each day's force in order that all the forces about you may become your loving helpers.

If you have more than one color in your birth digit, use the one which harmonizes with the force of the day.

Should you have but one color, such as gold, which expresses the first trinity 1, 2, 3, and the vibration of the day be pink, use the gold, as pink is composed of yellow, red and white, or use a salmon pink.

Should your force be gold, and the Queen of the Day be riding in her chariot of blue or green and you have no blue or green vibration, remember that this is not a good day for you to inaugurate activities. When possible spend such a day in reading or meditation, in this way storing up knowledge to be used at a time when nature is more conscious of your presence.

Seven neckties or gowns will serve to clothe you in cosmic harmony or you can use a variety of scarfs or veils.

The force of the day is Spirit, or at least it has spirit qualities. When it touches the earth it vitalizes the substances the sun is acting upon.

When different forces are in harmony, there is a perfect carnival of joyousness.

Is it not then wiser to join in the frolic rather than to let it pass by on the other side?

One cannot afford to sleep through this stage of activity. We came to earth to work and win experience upon all planes of life.

Suppose we illustrate our meaning by a few examples taken from the month of January, 1912.

January is month 1 and its influence extends through the entire month. It calls for creation and unity upon all planes of thought and action.

The year 1912 when added =

```
  1
  9
  1        3
  2        1
=13       =4
```

The digit of the entire year shows it to be one dominated by mental and physical force. This force will be felt during the entire year.

The color of 1–January–is flame and the color of the year's force is blue and green. The force of each separate day will make these colors either discordant or harmonious.

The force of the year, 4, is an individual one and rather difficult as a whole to fit into harmonious relations to other colors.

These two forces move the substances which are active during the entire month of January.

Jan. 1, 1912.

January Month 1	1
Day 1	1
Digit of year 1912	4

The combined force of January 1, 1912, is 6[32]. The digit of the other days can be found in the same manner.

Month	Day	Year	Force
1	1	4	6
1	2	4	7
1	3	4	8
1	4	4	9
1	5	4	1
1	6	4	11
1	7	4	3
1	8	4	4
1	9	4	5
1	10	4	6
1	11	4	5; 11
1	12	4	8
1	13	4	9
1	14	4	1
1	15	4	11
1	16	4	3
1	17	4	22
1	18	4	5
1	19	4	6
1	20	4	7
1	21	4	8
1	22	4	5; 22

32 4 + 1 + 1 = 6

1	23	4	1
1	24	4	11
1	25	4	3
1	26	4	4
1	27	5	6
1	28	6	6
1	29	5; 11	6
1	30	8	6
1	31	9	6

Jan. 1, 1912.

The vibration today is 1,1, 4. Its combined force is found by adding together the composition of the fundamental substances, 1, 1, 4, which we find to be 6.

This day will be acted upon by the 6 quality of force, which is set into action by the relative position of the earth to the sun.

Those working in the 6 force, as shown by the digit of the birth path, will find a harmony of action in all their undertakings if they will properly adjust themselves to its influence by using the force instead of allowing it to use them.

This applies equally to each day of the year; each day having its own peculiar force which moves the substances in harmony with it during each 24 hours. Take control of the force and act upon the substances and yourself control them, instead of being a substance and letting yourself be acted upon.

We will take two examples and try to clothe them harmoniously for a month.

Clara Horner was born Dec. 4, 1982.

	C = 3	
	L = 3	
Clara	A = 1	
	R = 9	1
	A = 1	7
	17	8

Keynote of Clara is 8. Color canary.

One-half of the system of Clara Horner has reached the 8 level of consciousness, which means a resurrected life.

	H = 8	
	O = 6	
Clara	R = 9	
	N = 5	
	E = 5	4
	R = 9	2
	42	6

The keynote of Horner is 6. Colors scarlet, heliotrope and orange.

Her level of consciousness is shown by adding 8, the digit of Clara, and 6, the digit of Horner, which gives 5. So it shows her level of consciousness.

She was born Dec. 4, 1892.

Dec. Month 12	digit 3
Day 1	4
Digit of year	2
Force	9

Colors red and brown.

The digit of her birth is 9. This is her working force and shows the quality of substances she will use in order to get her experiences.

To bring her sure results her own force should be in harmony with the force of the day, otherwise her energies will be inactive until a more harmonious concord appears.

Clara Horner's level of consciousness is not as high as the force she is working in, as Clara vibrates 8 and Horner 6, giving a digit of 5.

Her consciousness is limited and she is working in an unlimited vibration as found in the 9 of her birth path.

The 9 makes her give full expression to all phases of life; she dwells in the red and pink atmospheric lights, being fascinating, changeable and disobedient.

Love, with comes easily and goes easily. No matter into what depth she plunges, helping hands will clear her way, forgive her and love on, as her consciousness is pink, which means love without passion, while her birth number 9 gives her all the varieties of red from its purity to its dregs.

We will also analyze the number vibration of Sarah Katherine Foster.

	S = 1		
	A = 1		
Sarah	R = 9		
	A = 1	2	
	H = 8	0	
	20	2	

Add 2 + 0 to find the digit, which is 2.

This is the digit or keynote of Sarah. We say Sarah vibrates force 2. One-third of her system responds to the vibration of 2 and means, according to the chart, that she has conscious power of collecting knowledge of seen substances, but unless she is in accord with her trinity of 1, 2, 3, she is not willing to set the knowledge she has collected into action.

The color of 2 is gold. So Sarah and all No. 2's means a collection of cosmic forces.

Her mind pivots upon her middle name, Katherine, which vibrates 1. Thus:

	K = 2		
	A = 1		
	T = 2		
	H = 8		
Katherine	E = 5		
	R = 9		
	I = 9		
	N = 5	4	1
	E = 5	6	0
	46	10	1

As 46 is not a digit we add 4 + 6 to find 10.

1 color flame. 1 is a digit and shows the vibration or force of Katherine. The color of his name is flame. The point of attraction between herself and her parents is Foster.

This name vibrates 11.

	F = 6	
	O = 6	
Foster	S = 1	
	T = 2	
	E = 5	2
	R = 9	9
	29	11

11 colors, black, white, violet, yellow.

This part of her System tells us that she belongs to all nations and tribes. She is one of God's messengers and came to earth to aid one or many of the children of men. What she may do may seem trifling to the intellect, but in God's sight there is no great and no small. He sees only her willingness to serve not alone those she knows, but all souls.

She must deliver the message.

As 11 is outside of the regular gamut of number vibration, it is never added.

Sarah vibrates 2, color gold.

Katherine vibrates 1, color flame.

Foster vibrates 11, color black, white, yellow and violet.

Making her rate of consciousness 3; 11.

She holds in her system of conscious vibration, the concord 1, 2, 3; 11. This gives her a comprehensive sequence of thought and action.

She was born Dec. 1, 1892.

December is 12,	digit 3 substance.
First day	digit 1 substance.
Year 1892	digit 2 substance.
	= 6 Force.

Her birth force or vibration is 6, colors orange, scarlet and heliotrope.

This causes Sarah Katherine Foster to be closely related to the cosmic plane and fits her to meet life's demands in an independent manner, because she has displayed the trinity of action, 1, 2, 3, and her consciousness is higher than her birth force.

Her name contains an 11 and her birth force is 6. 6 is harmonious with 11 because the vowels of eleven equal 6, showing the harmony between the two planes.

11 represents the Creator Father and the 6 the Cosmic Mother, as it is 3 times 2.

On January 1, 1912, Force 6, Clara Horner, whose rate of consciousness is 5 and whose birth force is 9, should wear some shade of red for clothing, as there is scarlet in the air, and in any work which implies a fostering care she will meet success.

Sarah Katherine Foster, whose consciousness is 3; 11 and birth force 6, will find this day belongs to her if she will go forward to meet its benefits.

The force of the day is 6; her active force is 6.

She should wear one of the colors of the day, as the substances in which she will be successful are 1, 2, 3, and these represent a gold flame, while her own birth colors are orange, scarlet and heliotrope.

If she will wear some shade of gold or orange, these colors will laugh and rejoice in the sunshine.

Jan. 2, 1912.

1; 2; 4 = 7 Force.

Colors, purple, brick, steel.

Clara Horner, whose colors are red, brown and pink, and who sees things mainly through the tints of red, should wear on this day some shade of reddish purple, as this is a day when the fullness of earth and its shadows will be meet.

Sarah Katherine Foster, whose active force is 6–orange, scarlet and heliotrope–will be in complete harmony with herself and the Queen of nature in heliotrope garments, which will furnish the true point of contract.

Jan. 3, 1912.

1; 3; 4 = 8 Force.

Color, Canary.

Clara Horner, who sees things tinged with red, will find profit in considering the colors of the trinity she hopes to make, 8, 9, 11.

She is related to this trinity, as the 8 of her name shows, but has not yet fully arrived, as her name does not show the growth. She will do well to wear her own colors in golden shades.

Sarah Katherine Foster, who sees things through scarlet, orange and heliotrope, will find harmony between canary and the color of her birth force, orange.

Jan. 4, 1912.

1; 4; 4 = 9 Force.

Colors, red and brown.

The greater part of the children of men will find this day filled with extreme activity, bringing to light things hidden and it will be mingled with physical and mental disquietude.

Sarah Katherine Foster, with scarlet, orange and heliotrope colors, will find harmony today in a heliotrope gown, as the force of the day is red, while the substances acted upon are blue.

Clara Horner, whose force is red, will find that this day will further her projects in the business and mental world.

She should wear the red of her own force and keep it clear of the blue substances of the day, as it is composed of blue material and moved by the red force of a strong determined nature.

Today, if she will plant her feet firmly upon the truth as she knows it, with her arms in the world and her head in the ideal region, she will make a gain both for herself and the race.

Jan. 5, 1912.

1; 5; 4 = 1 Force.

Color, flame.

This day is entirely unlike yesterday. We find the message of the day to be, from its vibration, 1, 5, 4, = 1. "Find unity in life and sex upon both the mental and physical planes."

Today the atmosphere will burn with a flame of pink and blue.

Sarah Katherine Foster, who is moved by orange, scarlet and heliotrope, will find strength in garments of orange flame color.

Clara Horner, whose birth force is red, if she is inclined to inactivity, will find help in garments of pink shades, as pink is one of the substances moved today.

Jan. 6, 1912.

1; 6; 4 = 11 Force.

Colors, black, white, yellow, violet.

The message of the day, as told by the substances acted upon 1, 6, 4, is this: "The power of God will help him who strives to establish homes or in any way to give protection, as a mother would to those in need.

Action must be unity with the mental and physical law. The life of Jesus is in the vibration of this day.

Sarah Katherine Foster should wear either a yellow or white gown today.

Her surname Foster, which vibrates 11, shows that she can understand the need of today, manifesting the yellow principle, which is the principle of universality. This will be a day of value to this girl, because she can reach its vibration.

Clara Horner, will find this a difficult day to meet. All her problems will appear stupendous and she would do well to go quietly on her way without worrying over the mistakes she will make, simply trusting to the God principle within to guide her.

A purplish violet gown will help her today.

Jan. 7, 1912.

1; 7; 4 = 3 Force.

Color, a gold flame.

The message of the day as told by the substances moved, 1, 7, 4, with the 3 force, is: "Find unity in earth's fullness or its shadow will overpower you."

This is a day of physical and intellectual life, filled with thankfulness.

Sarah Katherine Foster, should wear a gown trimmed with yellow, as her individual force is orange and the day is yellow.

Clara Horne, whose life force is red and brown, will do well to wear tones of yellow brown.

Jan. 8, 1912.

1; 8; 4 = 4 Force.

Colors, blue and green.

The day's message, as found in 1, 8, 4 = 4, is a unity of resurrected action and thought. It is a day when difficult points can be gone over, argued upon and proved from a physical and mental basis.

Its colors are blue and green.

Sarah Katherine Foster should select from her own colors a heliotrope gown.

Clara Horner, working in red and brown, should wear combined brown and blue.

Jan. 9, 1912.

1; 9; 4 = 5 Force.

Color, pink.

The day's message as found in the substances moved is: "Give free soul expression to everything physical or mental. Life, love and sex will be prominent today."

Sarah Katherine Foster should select from her force of scarlet a pink garment in honor of the Queen of the day.

Clara Horner will understand this changeable, vacillating day. Within her system is a recollection of past turmoil's lived through. She, too, should wear pink. Messages from the past will come to her today.

Jan. 10, 1912.

1; 1; 4 = 6 Force.

Colors, orange, scarlet, heliotrope.

Sarah Katherine Foster will find this day especially valuable. Projects of all kinds will generate and things in general conspire to aid her. She should wear shades of yellow.

Clara Horner working in the red force, will also find this a harmonious day, as it contains the trinity 1, 2, 3, which her red force will frolic with. She should wear red or brown.

Jan. 11, 1912.

1; 11; 4 = 5 Force.

Color, pink.

The message of the day as told by the substances is to "unite the things of the spirit with things of the earth."

Today great projects will be started.

Sarah Katherine Foster should wear pink.

Clara Horner should wear pink bordering on red.

Jan. 12, 1912.

1; 3; 4 = 8 Force.

Color, canary.

The message of the day is "Go forward in all creative work." The forces present touch every point of body, soul and spirit on their own planes. A day for the resurrection of past memories and ideals.

Sarah Katherine Foster should wear yellow.

Clara Horner should wear yellow brown.

Jan. 13, 1912.

1; 4; 4 = 9 Force.

Colors, red and brown.

This is another day when the forces will urge to heights of joy or pain. A day when individual action and thought will surge forth overpoweringly.

It is a better day than it appears to be. The forces clash, but soon adjust themselves.

Sarah Katherine Foster should wear red.

Clara Horner should also wear red and try to realize that today she is working with her own forces.

Jan. 14, 1912.

1; 5; 4 = 1 Force.

Color, flame.

Today's message is to the natural man, "Spirituality sleeps to awaken in the morning."

This is a day when the colors speak in a manner difficult to understand.

To a mystic, pink is trying to assert itself over a green and blue foundation.

Sarah Katherine Foster will find cosmic harmony in a heliotrope gown.

Clara Horner may find in the heart of four whose value is 9. This shows that four has a red heart, as well as all mixed colors vibrating 9.

She will be in harmony in a gown of iridescent colors, as this also vibrates 4 and holds the red and pink in its composition.

Jan. 15, 1912.

1; 6; 4 = 11 Force.

Colors, black, white, yellow, violet.

This is a day bearing within its system of forces of golden opportunities for those who wish to advance in the journey of life toward the cycle of a perfect body, soul and spirit.

It holds the collected forces of the first trinity exalted to the highest relationship of it.

All the forces related to progress and their spiritual outcome are present today and need only the recognition and cooperation of man to become active for his use.

Sarah Katherine Foster will find this a perfect day for success and happiness, as her name, Foster, 11, relates her in consciousness to the high forms of this day.

Her birth force is 6, and as the vowels of eleven are of 6 value, this shows she is nestled in the heart of 11.

Like a frightened bird peeping over a high nest fearing the depths below, trusting only in the mother's care, so must a 6 trust an 11 when they are not related to 11 in name.

For Sarah Katherine Foster a dark blue or a violet dress will be harmonious.

Clara Horner, 9, will also find this a day of progress. A dark blue or red dress will be well chosen

Jan. 16, 1912.

1; 7; 4 = 3 Force.

Colors, gold, flame.

On this day conversation will abound upon intellectual subjects, but there will be a lack of harmony of action.

Sarah Katherine Foster will best hold the balance by wearing an abundance of yellow to represent her 2 force.

Clara Horner will be in harmony in dark brown and gold.

Jan. 17, 1912.

1; 8; 4 = 4 Force.

Colors, blue and green.

This is a day resulting in individual effort with flashes of light from a higher region. But the forces of the day urge to efforts for the individual rather than for the race.

Sarah Katherine Foster will do her best in dark blue or green.

Clara Horner will escape turmoil in brown, but will be more attractive in yellow or dark blue.

Jan. 18, 1912.

1; 9; 4 = 5 Force.

Color, pink.

This is a day when great forces of vibration are present in the earth and the impress of the day will be upon the world rather than upon the individual.

It is as changeable as a summer sky and equally as fascinating.

Sarah Katherine Foster will gladly harmonize this day with shades of pink.

Clara Horner should also wear pink.

Jan. 19, 1912.

1; 1; 4 = 6 Force.

Colors, orange, scarlet and heliotrope.

This is a day when the creative force will moan and groan in giving physical and mental birth to thoughts and actions.

Sarah Katherine Foster should wear heliotrope or orange.

Clara Horner, 9, should wear some shade of red.

Jan. 20, 1912.

1; 2; 4 = 7 Force.

Colors, purple, brick, steel.

This day will consist of a collection of past memories and events ending in an intellectual tumult. The day lacks complete expression.

Sarah Katherine Foster should wear purple.

Clara Horner, 9, should wear purple with some yellow.

Jan. 21, 1912.

1; 3; 4 = 8 Force.

Color, canary.

This day holds within its system of forces the complete unity of action and thought, 1, 2, 3. It is a day when great projects will be consummated in a cold, calculating manner. It is a canary day, holding within its system the memories of 2 and 4, gold and green.

Sarah Katherine Foster should wear tones of yellow.

Clara Horner, to succeed, should wear radiant shades of red.

Jan. 22, 1912.

1; 22; 4 = 5; 22 Force.

Colors, pink and cream.

This day abounds in the cream force of 22 and its companion, pink.

Many great projects will be quickly executed.

All life will be touched by the strong forces of creation.

Sarah Katherine Foster should wear cream.

Clara Horner should wear pink.

Jan. 23, 1912.

1; 5; 4 = 1 Force.

Color, flame.

This is a day when one is inclined to think and plan with little valuable action unless by effort one rises to the finer ether where currents have less effect. Then new creations may take form.

If the colors are held in the spiritual light, out of the discords of pink and blue, the result may be an unusual creation.

Sarah Katherine Foster should wear shades of yellow or pink.

Clara Horner should wear pink.

Jan. 24, 1912.

1; 6; 4 = 11 Force.

Colors, yellow, violet, black and white.

Today the first trinity is active, causing a sequence of thought and action.

The forces active are very human and will help everything that tends for the good of the race.

As the strength of today's forces combine in 11 and its meaning is told in black, white, yellow, violet, and as the individual force of Sarah Katherine Foster speaks through scarlet, orange and heliotrope, violet would be her harmonious color today.

Clara Horner, with an individual force of 9, red and brown, would best wear canary, the vibration of Clara, as there is no red in today's force.

Jan. 25, 1912.

1; 7; 4 = 3 Force.

Colors, gold, flame.

This is a day when people will talk solely on the intellectual plane. A full day for individual purposes.

Its highest color is a flame of purple, green and blue, burning with a golden glow.

Sarah Katherine Foster should wear light orange.

Clara Horner should wear golden brown.

Jan. 26, 1912.

1; 8; 4 = 4 Force.

Colors, blue and green.

This day speaks through blue and green. Intellectual and physical projects will be used for individual ends today.

Today things seen and not felt will win.

Sarah Katherine Foster will win today in dark blue or mulberry.

Clara Horner should select from the digit of her day of birth, dark blue or green.

Jan. 27, 1912.

1; 9; 4 = 5 Force.

Color, pink.

Today speaks through red, blue, green and pink.

It will bean active day in which, especially to those related to the 5 force, they unexpected will occur. And yet the day holds a good sequence of action.

Sarah Katherine Foster should wear shades of pink taken from the scarlet in her force.

Clara Horner should wear shades of red, as her controlling force is related to the force of the day.

Jan. 28, 1912.

1; 4; 4 = 6 Force.

Colors, orange, scarlet, heliotrope.

Today the force of 6 will move substances of equal value and will hold them and mother them until action is made perfect.

Sarah Katherine Foster will find in this a day in which nothing but a discordant brain will be able to block her success. She can wear any of her birth colors, as they are all present.

Clara Horner will find this a good day, but its events will

seem limited to her. She should wear some shade of red or a gold brown.

Jan. 29, 1912.

1; 11; 4 = 5 Force.

Colors, pink, black, white, violet and yellow.

This day lacks the power of expression and deals with all events in a highly mystical manner. But great and strong things will be consummated by those who hold to their highest ideals.

Sarah Katherine Foster will find herself strongly related to the events which will happen today. She will harmonize with a part of the force and with her individual force in pink.

Clara Horner should also wear tones of pink.

Jan. 30, 1912.

1; 3; 4 = 8 Force.

Canary is queen.

This day holds the sequence of thought and action of the first trinity of golden flame.

The force of the day is a strong canary light, helping everything to freedom and to free thought.

Sarah Katherine Foster should wear orange with touches of green or blue.

Clara Horner should work in accord with the trinity she is trying to make 8, 9, 11, and her own red tones will harmonize with the day's force of canary.

Jan. 31, 1912.

1; 4; 4 = 9 Force.

Colors, red and brown.

This will also be an unusually active day, filled full of physical and intellectual force.

In harmony will be present, but the force of the day represents the soul of the unseen, and by holding fast in thought to the Source of Life, the troubled earth waters will be stilled.

Sarah Katherine Foster will do well to wear heliotrope. Clara Horner will meet the events of this day as a queen, for the force of the day is her own individual force and all nature will conspire to help her.

She should wear some shade of red.

The Voice That Color Speaks

1–Flame.

2–Gold.

3–Gold Flame.

1, 2, 3, speak with a voice of unity in action and thought. Their combined symbol is a gold flame.

4–Blue and Green.

Blue means the presence of the foundation crystal of intellectual force. Green is the voice of seen things.

5–Pink.

Is the voice of the mystical holy Spirit of Life.

6–Scarlet, Orange, Heliotrope.

Each of these colors will help you hold and mother the cosmic force. Differing only in the colors that lie deeply concealed within their system, they are each a cosmic mother, which is the combination of both sex. Their vowels show the quality of action they contain. Scarlet is the same within as without, mothers and holds.

7–Purple.

Speaks the voice of the ages. That of royalty of blood and intellect; also through discords. From its heart it breathes in canary tones its desire for a physical resurrection.

8–Canary.

Speaks of a resurrected body still confined to earth and from within the message of a high, vibrating collection of all things from a gold center.

9–Red

This color speaks, claims and holds all life and all souls.

11–Black, White, Yellow and Violet.

Black holds at heart unexpressed unity. White holds and expresses all life and action upon all planes.

Yellow holds the highest and lowest equilibrium. Violet speaks the voice of the High Priest in language faintly understood.

22–Cream.

Asks you to cooperate with it in all things to benefit the race; its heart voice is the radiant colors of the cosmic mother.

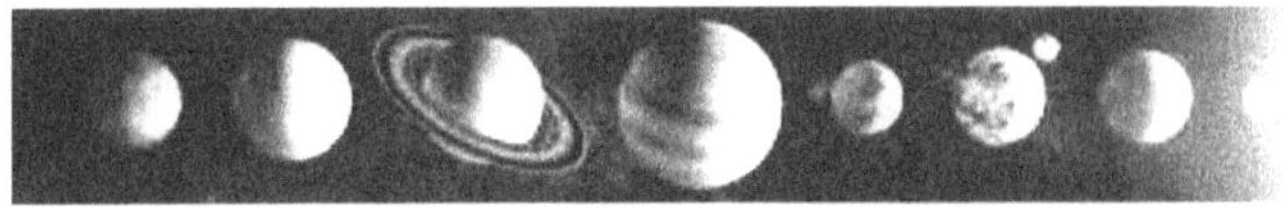

CHAPTER 5

The Music of the Spheres

A Lecture

What is the Music of the Spheres?

Made by each individual thing in the universe, be it world or man, striking its own note or sound. In that sound is the God principle which speaks for the soul of the thing.

In some parts of everything, from plant to man, from man to grain of sand,–in some part of the system of each thing is the quiet spot. In that spot is the closed door within which the soul of the thing dwells. Inside this door is the Holy of Holies and no man can enter. Even the most exalted thought can penetrate this place only a certain distance. It is the souls own and cannot be violated.

Every leaf of the forest has its note which is heard by the all-hearing ear and would also be heard by ours if we lived in conscious relation with the divine. We would hear the grass grown and hear the voice of all created things. This is true if we lived in tune with the infinite.

This music–the music of the spheres–is as our ears, as at present attuned, cannot hear the coarse sounds in the gamut below our normal hearing because our coarseness would disrupt our ears as the heat of the lower colors would blind our eyes, so the inharmony of certain notes cannot reach the ear of the advanced soul which is attuned too high for the discord of earth's voices to molest.

The untrained ear hears music through the emotion best fitted to express its soul's need, but the time will come when this same soul will hear far more than he hears now, for he will be able to distinguish the melody of each separate instrument joined in the harmony of the whole, and over crowning it will be the beautiful overtones, too fine for physical senses, unaided, to hear. These overtones are the voice of the soul.

What is meant in the Bible by the "Stars singing together," and "Voice of the flame," and "the floods clapping their hands?" Undoubtedly these expressions have a meaning, and this meaning must be found by their vibration, which means their outer form expressed to the intellect as number.

The question as to how each individual thing is related to color and tone can only be answered scientifically by going back to the sixth century before Christ. During that century Pythagoras gave to the ancient world his theory of music, which is regarded as the foundation of the musical system in use today.

With this system he also related individuals to tone and color and if one part of his system is true, all must be true, s they were developed from the same one source, the oneness and wholeness of the whole.

The world has never lost its belief in the teaching of this great philosopher and mystic, that the universe vibrates at different rates expressed by the digits of single numbers from 1 to 9. But the world failed to find the key to this great system, its very simplicity possibly darkening its meaning.

Many systems of numbers have been developed from different sources, the kabbalah, usually, being the basis. But every system has differed from every other system. This, as you know, has caused confusion and unbelief in the science of Number Vibration. I bring you a system of numbers that is as accurate and as scientific as the system of musical harmony in use today. It is founded, as all other systems are, upon the digits of numbers from 1 to 9. This is the correct teaching of Pythagoras, but from this point and finding the name and birth digit this system diverges from all the others.

The vibration of your name tells what you have accomplished in the past; it is the voice of past ages and reveals itself as character. It is the voice of the soul and tells what it desires you to know of your own strength or weakness. The soul cannot lie, as it is the essence and quality of your higher self. The intellect may try to deceive, but the soul never. It stands fairly for what it is, knowing it will in some future time make the perfect cycle of body, soul and spirit. When this is made, it will vibrate to the entire gamut of sound and color. Everything the eye sees or the ear hears will tell you its story if you but know how to understand its voice. The Bible story of our ancestor, Adam, naming the animals as they passed in review before him, is a correct test of vibration coming to us down the ages. As the animal passed Adam, its vibration spoke, and in an audible voice he give it the name fitted to express its then stage of development. As the animal advanced in development, its name may have changed, but it always expressed the stage of development at which the animal or thing had arrived at the time it was using the name.

If music has a scientific basis, then so has this system of number vibration, as it is built upon exactly the same foundation. Pythagoras, in the sixth century before Christ, gave to the world his theory of the Music of the Spheres when he gave to the Greeks the fundamental principles of music now in use. He taught that everything from a grain of sand to man was vibrating at its own rate of speed. If it had motion then it must have sound, if sound then it must have color. The rate of vibration must give the keynote of everything in the seen and unseen world.

Pythagoras taught that all vibrations in heaven and earth could be found in one of nine different paths of life. In order that the intellect might understand the teaching, he called the nine states numbers and made the paths of life vibrate from 1 to 9. In one of these nine vibrations you and I are trying to find that which our soul desires us to gain, and the sooner we gratify that wish of our higher self, the sooner will we realize the joy of life. This wish of our soul may seem to the intellect a very small thing, but remember, that in God's world there is no great and no small. There is not one of the life paths which does not contain enough joy and happiness to satisfy the soul if its laws are understood and met.

Every individual thing has its own rate of vibration and its own gamut of sound found in one of these paths which varies in length and intensity with the character and temperament.

A few ears are so attuned that they can function in the super-normal and there see colors and hear sounds which the average man says do not exist. This does not convince the man whose consciousness functions on the super-normal or cosmic plane that he does not hear sounds far transcending the ordinary gamut of sound.

We all possess this extended gamut of hearing but, before we can use it, there must be a lifting and lightening and listening quality of the body. To use it in the silence and lose it in the objective life is only to half realize that which is one's rightful inheritance.

When the eyes are opened to the high color vibrations and the ear can hear overtones, then will the race advance. When the public schools awaken to their responsibility, then will the dread of psychic phenomena be overcome. The state called psychic bears relation to but one part of the Trinity, and thus expresses a broken law which hinders development until its message to control and not submit is heard and heeded. There is no danger either in the seen or unseen to the soul who obeys law. We should always be masters instead of letting ourselves be controlled by any force whatever.

Our name represents our character. The character shows the soul's growth in the past and the Music of the Spheres is the music of all souls–the things of nature and of man–singing in harmony.

As different people are related to different planes on this earth, so are the ears of humanity attuned to hear different notes of the music of the spheres. The name shows that part we are unconsciously singing.

We cannot often hear its notes; in truth, we may be only striking one perfect note, which note is registered there, or it may be that all our notes are there but sounding in the lower realm, where they do not yet make perfect harmony. No one need fear to enter the realm of higher sight and sound if he banishes everything except trust in the Absolute.

If an individualized spirit with a name presents itself to consciousness and offers to guide, know that this is not a being from the higher realm, even though it declares itself the very son of the Supreme. Names are unknown in the realm of pure spirit and only the spirit which is universal and one with all mankind is a reliable guide.

When an individual is sufficiently advanced, he can relate himself to the Universal Plane and all the forces of good in the universe conspire to help him. But they can do no more than help. No good spirit ever tries to control a man. Invisible helpers assist the man who is master to mount to the Universal Realm, where all knowledge dwells and where man can learn truths which he can use to benefit the race.

When we cannot do this, we are living far below our birthright, for the Omniscient wishes us to know as He knows.

It is well for men to remember that it is quite as important for them to function perfectly upon the physical plane and to have perfect use of the objective intellect, as it is to function upon the higher planes you know. The proof of this is that the moment the soul so loses itself in the joys of the higher existence as to wish to cast off its body permanently in order to stay on the higher plane, that moment will the light be shut off and the soul will find itself with only the light of common day.

Every planet, star or sun has its own vibration, and as everything must have a center around which it revolves, it also has its key or dominant note around which all its other tones gather. The more spirit a thing contains, the higher is its rate of vibration.

When we spell out Jupiter, we find the digit to be 9, its vowels equaling 8, showing the planet Jupiter to be an advanced planet striking boldly the note of D in all the octaves. Its people, as shown by the vowels, are attuned to the 8 vibration and are a free, proud people singing in C.

The moon vibrates 3 and its people, when it had people, also vibrated 3. If the moon is a dead planet, it is because it has separated from its source. 3 is a part of the trinity 1, 2, 3, which must always work together. If it is not alive, it must have separated from the (one) 1 which is the spiritual or creative part. If we separate body, soul, and spirit, the expression of life is lost. In the same way when we separate 1, 2, 3, the expression is lost. If the moon is dead, it is controlled by forces which now express more life. So with the individual who vibrates 3,–and there are very many of them–when he is separated from the creative force he is no more than a moon shining by reflected light. The thing that vitalizes a planet is the spiritual life of its inhabitants. As the moon is now dead, it remains as a monument of life of the past.

Each of the twelve constellations is composed of many stars or suns giving out light which some have dared to suggest emanates from the souls of men. As God chose fire as a symbol of his spirit and as musical vibration is designated by number, so amid all the stars of each constellation, one especial planet seems especially related to that constellation. As each constellation differs as a whole from the others, so must each individual star of the constellation differ in its note. But the keynote of the constellation is the combined voice of the whole. When we know where we belong among the starry constellations of golden gems which adorn the canopy above, we must look to see what planet rules or is located in the constellation.

We find that five constellations have reached a free note, and in the chorus of the spheres can take up any C in any octave of the gamut of sound, Jupiter and Venus always sounding D.

Any planet found in the constellation of Aquarius, Sagittarius, Pisces, Virgo, or Cancer has the advantage of a broad outlook, even though it may itself be limited. From its situation it has a power of growth the other planets do not have. When you go through different states in our own country or in foreign lands, you see that the soil differs in different places, so it is with these planets; they have a sense of freedom unknown to the other constellations.

Sagittarius and Pisces are the strongest of all the constellations, as both of these vibrate 8 and each is ruled by Jupiter, who vibrates even higher than the constellations themselves.

Jupiter and Venus are the two human, soulful planets in our chain, as both vibrate 9 and their people 8, two high free numbers. These planets are able to strike two full, free notes C and D. No wonder we regard Jupiter and Venus as powers of might Sagittarius and Pisces are blessed in having Jupiter as their ruler.

Aquarius has the same form of freedom as Sagittarius and Pisces and is, therefore, striking the same free note of C in any octave, but its ruler, Saturn, is of uncertain quality. Saturn has the 3 vibration and its people 4, which make it of inharmonious quality.

Aquarius people are apt to be mystical and negative and so have clairvoyant power; but as they are controlled by the planet Saturn, which vibrates 3, 4, an opposite quality to that expressed by the free 8, the people in this sign are often torn asunder by opposing desires, as the inhabitants are as strongly related to physical as to spiritual force. For this reason we often find Aquarius people balancing between two forces, but their free constellation always gives them a certain dignity even in their weakness.

Virgo also strikes the fundamental note of C, meaning freedom. Its ruling planet is Mercury. This planet is not of high vibration, as it strikes the limited note F in just one octave. The inhabitants of Virgo are in accord with the constellation, but they have outgrown the planet.

Cancer is the last of the constellations able to strike the note that belongs to the highest trinity of harmony. Cancer is governed by the Moon, which vibrates 3, and may either show a changeable quality or be a great aid in complete spiritual expression.

Scorpio is the constellation which deals with life and sex. It strikes G, the fifth note, its people, 3, may either express the great truth of Unity or scatter and destroy. Its planet is Mars, who has been called the God of War. At its highest Mars is a beautiful cosmic mother of unity.

Leo also vibrates 5, like Scorpio, and deals with sex and life in all its forms. But its people, unlike those of Scorpio, aim to reach the highest and grasp the full octave of C. The free spirit of the people of this sign is assisted by their ruler, the sun.

All the other constellations we find striking notes less bold and clear than Aquarius, Sagittarius, Pisces, Virgo, and Cancer.

We find Taurus, Gemini, Capricorn, Aries, Libra, Scorpio and Leo to be less developed constellations, but the same planets rule them.

One need not be ruled by the stars, but it makes life easier when we know their tone and consciously work with them harmonizing all the forces. Then we can use their force and they cease to use us.

Some things have weak voices as we judge weak and strong. But remember, we must not judge anything by the place it seems to occupy in the seen world.

Great men often walk among us unrecognized, working in humble callings and appearing very ordinary people, when if our ears were opened we should hear them singing great octaves on the unseen side of life.

The sparrow and cedar bird vibrate, the one n and the other 22, the highest of seen forms, and respond respectively to the entire octave of C and D, although on this, the seen side of life, their songs are not heard; while the canary, bobolink and mockingbird, although vibrating in the gamut of free expression, have only one free note and not an octave of sound like the others. And yet we say the mockingbird is a singer and the other is not.

The violet, camellia, lily and daisy have a whole octave of sound. A dog, a chicken and a lamb strike a free note and are related to the spiritual trinity. A horse vibrates 11, showing it to be the highest seen form.

An automobile vibrates 5, its voice being 3. Thus there is an harmonious relation in it structure. Milk, beef, bacon, strike a free note, as does anything smoked. Mutton and cream vibrate to a full octave of sound.

The thing with the highest vibration is not the thing most loved by the masses. For instance, the closemouthed clam is vibrating to a whole octave of sound on the unseen side, that side on which there is no high and no low, but only darkness and light, the negative and the positive. In contrast to the highly vibrating clam, beloved of the few, the oyster, which is an almost universal food, vibrates 4. This appeals to the intellectual and physical nature and its one note, F, any man can reach; while comparatively few can follow the clam into its octave. The clam is never at any season unhealthy, for it vibration is too high for disease to reach when it understands how to use its note to restore equilibrium.

If we understood life's song, our song, found from birth number, other's song, and understood that our song would go on throughout the eternities, we would be more patient with the brother who has faltered by the way and who yet, notwithstanding his uncertain steps, may be making for himself an octave of sound far more clear and beautiful than our own.

If we could realize that when the earth dust drops from our eyes and ears, we will hear with the ears of the spirit, and as we have passed the gamut of notes below us, which has less rhythmic melody and harmony than the one we now hear, so we will finally come to hear all creation singing together, when the thunder blast, the voice of the worm and the octaves of man blend in one mighty chorus in which only our perfected notes are heard, we would be more willing to help the backward brother to get his note clear.

When we know all voices are one voice, all colors are one color, and that all things are different expressions of the one in different tones and keys, we then cease to see through a glass darkly but know as children of light.

Your system of body, soul, and spirit has a keynote which is made intelligible to your intellect as number. This is the keynote in which you are singing your song of life. When you started out upon life's journey, in order to make a perfect expression of body, soul, and spirit, you struck some note. Every victory made on the side of right added something to your song, and if you have progressed sufficiently, you are now singing a full octave in Nature's chorus.

If everything is in a state of vibration, then everything must take its part in the great choir. If every created thing did not join, then the law of the universe would be broken and chaos and disruption would reign.

How many people in listening to a fine orchestra can hear the overtones? Very few; and yet overtones belong to the physical plane, to the highest part of the physical, and are within the power of any individual to hear. When a person really desires to hear the highest tones that can be produced all nature conspires to help him. So, as you listen to a band playing full harmonics, listen to the reproduction of the sound above the normal gamut. There will be a separation of sounds, the instruments will still be playing but when your body gets sufficient of the listening quality, above the silence you will hear another band striking notes, silvery and harmonious. These are the overtones, the spiritual part of the harmony made by the musicians below. It will be easier for us to hear overtones in music played in the keynote of our birth path.

While overtones belong to the physical plane, astral music belongs in the plane above the physical or what is called the astral plane. Astral music closely resembles music heard on the physical plane, but the man who listens to it will be surprised to find that he never hears a familiar tune. He is like on listening to the music of a strange country. The ability to hear astral music may come from an ardent desire to hear astral sounds; but the power to hear never comes with the desire. When the ardent desire has ceased to be positive; the power to hear may come.

But it always comes as a gift and not with effort. Astral music is heard in the silence and the tones seem to be finer and thinner than the music of the physical plane.

I would not talk to you of these things if I had not myself actually experienced them. I would not teach these things if when in doubt as to their reality the Great Father had not unsealed my eyes and unstopped my ears until I saw and understood why many things not comprehended before must exist in life's endless progress. Did I hear these things through the psychic senses? No; but through the unlocking of my spiritual faculties in order that I might help fellow travellers.

The first time I heard the Music of the Spheres I was in a sleeping car, the best place in the world, except a boiler shop, to find the true silence. When my head first touched the pillow I was conscious of the grating, grind and thud of the wheels beneath me. Then came stillness and listening, I heard the grating sounds grow finer, softer, until by and by the sounds separated, everything seeming to be enveloped in the gray mist. Then to my surprise I began to hear faint glorious music of a kind I never heard before. It arose as if from the depth of earth and sea, silvery, watery, fiery, and the unity of the whole so blended that it filled me with awe. I arose and sat upon the side of my berth, while the grandeur and majesty of the song rolled on and I seemed constantly able to hear more and more from the finest highest notes down to the thundering bass. Unlike earthly music it had no melody, but the mighty harmony rolled on and on unceasing.

Then my prayer went up to the Great Choir Master to let me hear more–more–more, only to hear. I was willing to give up my body in order to hear more.

Instantly the song ceased and I could hear nothing but the grinding of the car. The following days I prayed as only an ardent soul can to hear the music once more. Then while about my daily work the Heavens again opened and I heard once more the same song. Still later, for the third time, I heard the voice of the worlds and then I knew I should never hear it again until I stood with eyes and ears no longer hindered with earth's dust.

The Master wastes no force, but when especial help is needed to do especial work, if we cling close to the source, the help is always given.

When we ask, What is music? We find it defined in the Encyclopedia Britannica "As the art that employs sound as a medium of artistic expression for what IS NOT in the province of literature whether in verse or prose; what is not in sculpture, painting, acting or architecture. Literature portrays states of emotion, sculpture imitates the outward forms of animate things, whereas painting vitalizes with color the forms of sculpture and extends its range of subjects not only to animate, but to inanimate nature. Acting gives the mobility of life to sculpture, which is an imitation. Music embodies the inward feeling of which all those other arts can but exhibit the effect.

Music has an analogy to architecture which it has not to the other fine arts, as it makes but conventional reference to nature in the lines and the lights and shadows of the natural world–in this particular music has an analogy to architecture which it has not to the other fine arts. In the matter of expression also architecture may be compared to music in the earlier stages of its development, but music left architecture far behind when in later days it assumed the power of special individual and personal expression of every variety of passion. Music embodies the inward feeling of which all those other arts can but exhibit the effect.

This proves music to be one of the great realities and all other arts but imitations. Music uses the other arts somewhat as the soul uses the body, which is to assist it to advance in its great journey towards perfection. Some have called music the universal language. The same authority quoted says, the definition is not true and gives us a reason that in every age and clime there are varieties of musical idiom which are unsympathetic, if not unintelligible, to other generations than those with whom they were first current; and still more, the very principles that govern it have been and are so variously developed at different times and places that music which is delightful to one people, is repugnant at another epoch or to a different community.

If music is that art which embodies the inward feeling of which all the other arts are imitations, in outward form, then music must stand as the soul of all seen things. It emerges from the quiet spot in your system and in mine where the spark of the Absolute dwells. As it moves forth into the seen world it causes motion, which causes sound; sound turns to tone and tone to color, and color to the reflection of all colors in one harmonious perfect white. All the sounds and notes are still present, but the ear of man is not attuned to their spiritual quality, although on the other side, the unseen side, they are not registered as the music of the spheres.

Colors, then, are not expressions of different state of vibration vitalized as music, the different colors showing what note is being struck, and how much spirit is being expressed. Music is the interpreter of color and endows color with life. Color touches the individual through the sense world, and music interprets the feeling aroused.

Science tells us there is but one true color, the ultramarine, which, being impervious to fire is found in the volcano. Its vibration is 6, showing it to be a cosmic mother. The digit of its vowels is 1, showing it to be the principle of unity. All other colors are mixtures, like the blood of the races; yet, perhaps, there may be one race which, like the ultramarine, stands for the quiet spot whose note is purity.

It is not absolutely necessary that we should be surrounded by the colors of our own vibration any more than it is necessary for us to walk to march time. We can go through life trying to keep step to waltz time instead of to the 4-4 time, suitable for walking. But as it is easier to walk to 4-4 time, so it easier for us when the colors around us vibrate to the keynote of our birth digit. Most of us possess two dominant colors, our name color and our birth color, and we should be as familiar with them as with the face of a friend.

Red, in all shades, has the power of complete expression when the form that expresses this wondrous color knows how to strike its free note D. It is a color much abused and is often by coarse natures made to strike its beautiful note in a very low octave.

The color, red, is so rich and free in its own vibration, so typical of the blood of the race, that it has the power to express either purity or vice as no other color can. The harlot may with propriety wrap around herself a cloak of various shades of red, and the young mother may with equal propriety cover her child with a coverlet of the same hue. But the mother strikes the note in a high octave, while the harlot sounds it in a lower one; but it is always the note D singing the same song for all the red clad souls.

When we take red and fill it with the white rays until it blushes from red to pink, we find its outer form expresses less strength, but internally it is the same.

It strikes the same note, but is bound by another dominant note that hampers it and holds it within the limits of the earth's boundaries, called life. As we see it, pink strikes the note of G and means love without passion. It is life's color.

The reason that blue and green are more used for clothing and house furnishing than other colors, is because these colors vibrate 4, which expresses the individual alone. To bring either into a higher vibration so as to meet the needs of all humanity, one must add a secondary and higher principle. Anybody can understand the vibration of blue or green, which is the reason they are always popular, changing only in degree, never in foundation. When we add "light" to blue, we add the highest of all vibrations, the spiritual 11.

When we add "white" or "light" to any color we add a whole gamut of colors and give it the use of a whole octave of sound. When we add dark and light to any color, we strengthen its vibration. But as "light blue" continues to contain within its system the 4 principle–the single note of F in one octave–it will express less freedom than "dark blue," where the 4 principle loses its strong physical and intellectual character in the freedom of the unseen. Dark blue (7 + 4 = 11) is higher in vibration than "light" (11, 4). "Light blue is higher than medium blue, which is the color of the masses and speaks for the individual and not for the race. The lower its vibration, the less enduring its lasting quality.

Green vibrates the same note as blue. This is a green earth, and the green of earth and the blue of sky blend inharmoniously unless a spiritual quality is added either as "dark" or "light." Then the weary soul can grasp the shade to which it is attuned and with no mental effort the colors of blue and green will fit into his life. The green of the earth, greenbacks, and silver, all strike the same note of F.

Outwardly, orange vibrates 6 and strikes the note of A. 6 shows it to be a cosmic mother, but it shows strength in a limited condition. It is a strong color because its internal structure is much stronger than its outward form, and as the internal structure of 6 is 11, there is perfect concord between its outward and its inner forms.

Yellow and violet, with white, black and cream are expressing whole octaves of sound. In these colors is expressed every emotion the human heart is capable of feeling.

Yellow is more closely related to the soul than other colors as its mission is to collect, to gather, to arrange, to give out. This is especially true of the shade known as gold, which is the drawing together color. When this color lacks the luminosity which the flame of spirit gives, it is negative and an earth color. With the spiritual quality added it belongs to all colors and is no longer confined to the trinity of mind known as 1, 2, 3.

It is no sin to possess gold, but to take it from the cosmic store-house, to which all have access, and to hoard it and hide it in values, is to remove it from its source and to reduce it to nothing but the mineral gold, where it strikes but one note in one octave, D. It is not so with yellow, which laughs and rests in freedom of God's love and strikes all the notes in the whole gamut of sound.

Within the colors of white, yellow, violet and cream, as well as black, abides the power to express every harmony, every emotion, every architectural structure, all sculpture, every color that is spread on any canvas, every song a bird can sing, the noise of the waterfall, the thunder's roar–these are all expressed in white, yellow, violet and cream.

Violet, as you know, is a borrowed color and belongs in the gamut above the one the natural eye sees.

But someone who has seen has reproduced its shade in form and the whole octave of sound has flowed into it.

Black means the absorption of all sounds and colors. It holds within its sombre folds every emotion, color, and note known to mortals, but it is negative and fails to reflect, and while hugging its treasures fails to realize their brightness. Black holds as much as white; but while black is negative and absorbs.

White is and gives out. White gives freely as God gives, to all men, and we can find the echo of every note in the world's great chorus, every color in the rainbow, in the pure white light. It is the color to use for healing and contains within its consciousness all the wealth of the universe.

Fire and water vibrate whole octaves of sound. It is true the flame can sing any melody the listening ear can hear.

It is true, if one will listen to the ocean's roar he can hear every instrument ever used in an orchestra; they are all there and only need the hearing ear to bring them to consciousness. You can find in water every color the eye ever saw or the mind imagined.

They are all there merely waiting for you to bring them forth.

As every soul that walks the earth has his mission and message, so has each individual color and note its message.

In every note there are three distinct planes of tone, and so in color we find the same law. As every soul has some good in it, so is every color good, in its time and place. Somewhere in its system is the quiet spot where the language of the soul speaks, and will speak to you if you have ears to hear.

Through vibration comes motion, through motion comes color, through color comes tone. Music used these forces and amidst their universal action it sorts and sifts from the inharmonious, harmonies, placing them exactly where the Great Choir Master desires to them to be. Not one thing is forgotten; everything is there and each thing has its rightful place in the music all are making.

As below, so above. If everything has its quiet spot where God abides, then this spot will be found in the overtone which seems almost too high for mortal ear. Possibly our present overtones may be the music of our future state, and above them will be a still finer overtone until we go on and on until sound ceases and we dwell in a world beyond the Music of the Spheres when spiritual man may himself be the musical expression of the Absolute.